YAS

FRIENDS
OF ACPL

EVERYDAY LIFE IN
Medieval Europe

BY
KATHRYN HINDS

 **Marshall Cavendish**
Benchmark
New York

The author and publishers would like to thank Alexandra Service, PhD, Medieval Studies, University of York, England, for her assistance in reading the manuscript.

The oath of homage on pp. 12–13 is quoted from Oliver I. Thatcher and Edgar H. Macneal, eds., *A Source Book for Medieval History*, NY, 1905, pp. 364–365. The games on pp. 50, 119, and 177 are adapted from *Medieval Holidays and Festivals* by Madeleine Pelner Cosman. The recipe on p. 61 is adapted from *Fabulous Feasts* by Madeleine Pelner Cosman. The translation of "Non es meravelha s'eu chan" on p. 65 is by Kathryn Hinds. The population figures on p. 76 are from *Life in a Medieval City* by Frances Gies and Joseph Gies. The recipes on p. 99 are adapted from *The Medieval Kitchen* by Odile Redon et al. and *Gode Cookery* by James L. Matterer. The translation from *Yvain* on p. 111 is by Kathryn Hinds. The translations/adaptations of Middle English songs and poems on pp. 123, 181, and 186–187 are by Kathryn Hinds. "The Song of Brother Sun" on p. 227 is adapted from "The Canticle of Brother Sun" in *Francis and Clare: The Complete Works*, translated by Regis J. Armstrong and Ignatius C. Brady. The quotations from the Rule of Saint Benedict on pp. 252 and 255–256 are from the translation by Rev. Boniface Verheyen, OSB. All translations/adaptations from *The Canterbury Tales* are by Kathryn Hinds. All biblical quotations are from The Holy Bible, Revised Standard Version.

EDITOR: JOYCE STANTON   PUBLISHER: MICHELLE BISSON
ART DIRECTOR: ANAHID HAMPARIAN   SERIES DESIGNER: JEAN KRULIS

Printed in Malaysia
135642

Front cover: A farmyard scene painted by Simon Bening (1483–1561), from the *Da Costa Book of Hours*
Title page: Sowing the fields in October, from the *Playfair Book of Hours*, made in France in the late fifteenth century.
Back cover: Saint Mark writing in his study, by Simon Bening, from the *Da Costa Book of Hours*

Contents

ABOUT THE MIDDLE AGES

When we talk about the Middle Ages, we are talking about the period of European history from roughly 500 to 1500. Toward the end of this time, Italian scholars and writers known as humanists began to take a new interest in the literature and ideas of ancient Greece and Rome. The humanists wanted to create a renaissance, or rebirth, of ancient learning. They believed they were living in a new age, with a culture that was far superior to the culture of the previous ten centuries. So they called the years between the fall of Rome and their own time the Middle Ages, and the name has stuck.

The Italian humanists thought that the Middle Ages were dark, barbaric, ignorant, and without any kind of human progress. Today we often think of medieval times as a kind of storybook never-never land, with bold knights riding out on quests, jesters and wandering minstrels entertaining at sumptuous banquets, and kings and queens ruling from towered castles. But the real story about the Middle Ages is more fascinating than any fairy tale.

Just like life today, life in medieval times was full of complexity and variety. Most people were peasants who spent their lives farming in the countryside, but cities were growing and becoming increasingly important. Numerous women and men devoted themselves to religion, spending their lives serving in the Church. And of course there were castles, homes to kings, queens, nobles, and knights—and to large numbers of servants and craftspeople as well.

Medieval people had many of the same joys and sorrows, hopes and fears that we do, but their world was very different from ours. Forget about telephones, newspapers, computers, cars, and televisions. Step back into time, into the years 1100 through 1400, the High Middle Ages. Let history come alive. . . .

THE CASTLE

1
LOYALTY AND PROTECTION

For hundreds of years, much of Europe was part of the Roman Empire. The rest of the continent was controlled by various tribal peoples, whom the Romans referred to as barbarians. When Rome fell to barbarian invaders in the fifth century, Europe was left with no central government, administration, or defense. Power was held by those who controlled the most land and who commanded the strongest forces of warriors. Europe's great landowners held sway over many small realms and were frequently at war with one another.

The lack of unity paved the way for invasions. During the eighth century Muslim warriors attacked from the east and south. They took over most of what is now Spain, much of which remained in Muslim hands for hundreds of years.

The conquerors were prevented from reaching farther into Europe by the Franks, a powerful tribe (from whom France takes its name). The Franks had recently developed a new style of warfare, which depended on troops of heavily armed warriors on horseback—knights. This knightly warfare led to other developments: To get and hold power, a ruler needed the services and loyalty of

French knights riding to battle during the fourteenth century. In their right hands they hold their lances, banners flying. On their chests they carry their shields. Each shield bears the knight's coat of arms, a design that belonged to him alone and was a way for other knights to identify him on the battlefield.

many knights. In return for their loyalty, the ruler rewarded them with land and privileges. Men with the wealth to afford horses and equipment therefore rose in importance and power themselves, often becoming great nobles.

The greatest of the Frankish kings, Charlemagne (SHAR-luh-mane), took full advantage of these developments and united most of western Europe into a single empire. With the knights he commanded and the fortresses he built, Charlemagne was able to defend his empire well. It survived many attacks by the Muslims and also by the Vikings, who had begun to make frequent raids on western Europe's towns and villages. When Charlemagne died in 814, his empire quickly fell apart. But the kings who came after him followed his example in relying on knightly warfare. Many customs grew up around this style of warfare, giving shape to the system now known as feudalism (FYOO-duh-lizm).

LORDS AND VASSALS

Feudalism was a military and political arrangement among kings and noblemen. By the High Middle Ages it had spread throughout much of western Europe and was particularly strong in France, England, and Germany. Its details varied from place to place, and in some areas, such as Scandinavia, it did not take hold at all. Wherever feudalism existed, however, its outline was basically the same.

In theory, a king owned all of the land in his kingdom. He kept a large portion of the land for his own use, and a great deal of land was also held by the Church. The king granted the use of the rest of the land to his vassals, the nobles who were his most powerful supporters. In return for these land grants, called fiefs, the vassals owed the king military service. They acknowledged the king as their lord, pledging to fight for him in person and also to provide a certain number of knights in time of war.

The king's vassals granted portions of their lands to lower-ranking nobles who, in return, promised knightly service. And just as the king's vassals had vassals of their own, these men, too, might take on vassals.

In addition to military service, vassals of all ranks had various other duties to their lords. These included escorting the lord on his travels, guarding his castle, and always being ready to welcome a visit from him. The lord had the right to summon his vassals to a council at any time. Vassals were usually expected to make money payments to the lord on certain occasions: when the lord granted them fiefs, when the lord's oldest daughter got married, and when his oldest son became a knight. If the lord was taken prisoner by an enemy, his vassals were required to pay ransom money to free him.

Beginning in the twelfth century, vassals who paid a tax called scutage did not have to perform military service for the lord. He used the tax money to hire mercenary soldiers instead. (Lords often preferred this—a vassal was only required to fight for the lord for forty days a year, but a hired soldier would serve the lord for as long as he was paid.)

The feudal bond was cemented by a ceremony in which the lord swore to protect and defend the vassal, and the vassal swore lifelong loyalty to the lord. This loyalty was not always upheld, however—royal vassals in particular rose in rebellion against their king quite often throughout the High Middle Ages.

The king and queen of France, Jean le Bon ("the Good") and Jeanne de Boulogne, ride into Paris. They are accompanied by their many servants, vassals, and other retainers. Jean le Bon ruled from 1350 to 1364.

THE CEREMONY OF HOMAGE: A VASSAL'S VOWS

The great hall of the lord's castle is crowded with knights, ladies, and members of the lord's household. There is an expectant silence in the room as all eyes are turned on the lord and his new vassal. With a great sense of importance and seriousness, lord and vassal face each other. The vassal kneels before the lord, and the lord takes the vassal's clasped hands between his own. In this position, the vassal swears to aid the lord, and the lord formally grants fiefs (lands) to the vassal and swears to aid him in turn. The oaths are sealed with a ceremonial kiss.

This was homage, the ceremony that cemented the relationship between lord and vassal. Whenever a vassal took possession of land, he was required to do homage—or honor—to the lord. When a lord acquired new lands, he expected to receive homage from all the vassals on those lands.

Feudal relationships could be very complicated. A vassal might hold lands from more than one overlord. Sometimes the king of one country was even the vassal of the king of another country. England's Henry II, for example, had large landholdings in France, for which he was a vassal to the French king. The following thirteenth-century statement of homage reflects this kind of complexity:

> I, John of Toul, make known that I am the liege man of the lady Beatrice, countess of Troyes, and of her son, Theobald, count of Champagne, against every creature, living or dead, saving my allegiance to lord Enjorand of Coucy, lord

John of Arcis, and the count of Grandpré. If it should happen that the count of Grandpré should be at war with the countess and count of Champagne on his own quarrel, I will aid the count of Grandpré in my own person, and will send to the count and the countess of Champagne the knights whose service I owe to them for the fief which I hold of them. But if the count of Grandpré shall make war on the countess and the count of Champagne on behalf of his friends and not in his own quarrel, I will aid in my own person the countess and count of Champagne, and will send one knight to the count of Grandpré for the service which I owe him for the fief which I hold of him, but I will not go myself into the territory of the count of Grandpré to make war on him.

2
FEUDAL FORTRESSES

Ⓣhe greatest symbol of feudal life was the castle. In the 800s castles were being built all over what are now France, the Netherlands, Germany, and Italy. When William the Conqueror invaded England in 1066, he took with him an enthusiasm for castle building. In 1066 there were only half a dozen castles in England; by 1100 there were more than five hundred.

The castle was a protection against attackers and a center of power. Kings and lords used their castles to defend as well as to extend their territory. For example, after William the Conqueror's invasion of England, he faced many rebellions. Upon ending each one, he promptly ordered a castle to be built on the site of the rebellion. After that, the local people were firmly under his control. This tactic was valuable to many later kings and conquerors, too. In the thirteenth century King Edward I ringed Wales with some of the mightiest castles in Europe, using the strength of these fortresses to bring the Welsh under English rule.

STRONG DEFENSES

The earliest European castles were usually a type called motte-and-bailey. Castle builders made a huge, steep, earthen mound—the motte (MAHT)—surrounded by a deep ditch. Around the top of the mound they erected a timber palisade, or wall. Within the wall was a stronghold called a keep or donjon, typically a tall, wooden, rectangular tower. Below the motte there was a large area enclosed by its own ditch and palisade. This was the bailey. Usually the castle's commander and his family lived in the keep, and his soldiers, with their horses and supplies, were housed in buildings in the bailey. In an emergency, everyone could go to the motte and the keep for safety.

Around 1100 most European castles were still constructed of wood. But during the next hundred years nearly all castles were built or rebuilt in stone. At some motte-and-bailey castles the palisade atop the motte was replaced by a high stone wall. At other places the bailey received the new fortifications, with a rectangular stone keep being placed within a very thick stone curtain wall.

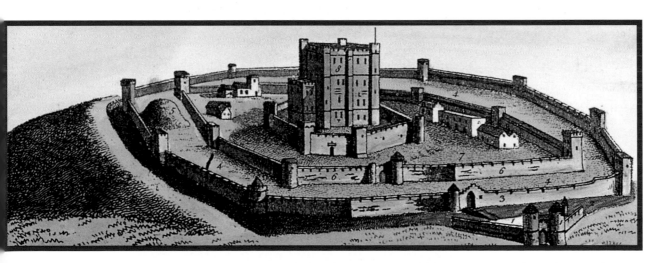

A typical English castle of the eleventh or twelfth century, with 1) the gatehouse, 2) the ditch or moat, 3) the outer curtain wall, 4) the outer bailey, or courtyard, 5) an artificial mound, which may have served as an extra lookout point, 6) the inner curtain wall, 7) the inner bailey, and 8) the keep, which is built on top of a low motte, or mound.

A twelfth-century stone castle in Montbrun, France. The outer curtain wall is extremely high and is fortified by strong round towers. The square towers of earlier castles had a drawback: attackers could hide in their angles.

The curtain was also used for completely new castles, and it gave Europe's feudal fortresses their distinctive "square-toothed" look. The top of the curtain was typically crenellated (KREH-nuh-lay-ted)—that is, it had alternating square or rectangular high and low sections. Each high section had an arrow loop, a narrow opening through which archers could shoot at attackers. At each low section, castle defenders could reach out to drop heavy stones, boiling liquids, and the like upon their enemies. The archers and other defenders stood on stone walkways built along the wall.

The curtain also had several towers, usually at the corners and at various points along the wall's length. At first the towers were rectangular, but later castle builders preferred round towers, which were easier to defend. From the towers the castle's soldiers could keep an eye on every part of the wall.

Since troops of warriors, as well as individuals, needed to be able to enter and leave the castle, there had to be one or two large doorways in the wall. These were vulnerable points, so they were heavily fortified with strong gatehouses. A gatehouse was made up of two massive towers, one on each side of the doorway, and a number of barriers. The first barrier was often a drawbridge over a ditch. (The ditch later came to be called the moat.) The drawbridge was raised in times of danger. Then there was a kind of gate called a portcullis. Beyond this was a set of heavy oak doors reinforced with iron bands. A stout wooden bar across the entryway made a final barrier. Some castles had two portcullises, two sets of doors, and two bars for an even stronger defense. By the thirteenth century, when castle building was at a peak, many castles were also given two curtain walls, one surrounding the other.

INSIDE THE WALLS

At the simplest castles, a keep was the major building, with a storage area on the ground floor, a great hall above it, and living quarters on the top floor. Later, more elaborate castles had a number of buildings behind their curtain walls. The largest structure was the great hall, where the lord held court.

Early on, all the residents of the castle slept in the great hall. The lord and lady had some privacy behind a curtain or partition at

CASTLE COMFORTS

If you were to tour the ruins of a medieval castle, you would probably find it difficult to imagine anyone living in such a bare stone building. But these castles looked very different during the Middle Ages. Their outside walls were often whitewashed, so that they almost gleamed in the sunlight. Inside walls might be whitewashed as well. In the great hall and the nobles' chambers, the walls were frequently paneled with wood, painted (white, or in colors such as green and gold), and even embellished with murals. Hangings of painted cloth provided more decoration and helped cut down on drafts. In the fourteenth century tapestries, elaborately woven pictures, became popular wall coverings in castles all over Europe. Floors during this period, however, were generally bare wood or stone, strewn with sweet-smelling rushes and herbs.

The upper floors of castle buildings sometimes boasted large windows with glass panes. Often there was a cushioned window seat, where a lord or lady might sit comfortably—to enjoy a view of the castle garden, or to take advantage of the natural light in order to read, do needlework, and the like. Other lighting was supplied by candles (made from animal fat or, more expensively, beeswax) and oil lamps. A twelfth-century invention, the fireplace, provided both light and heat. Set into the wall so that the surrounding stones radiated heat, the fireplace was a great improvement over the central hearths of the past.

High, curtained beds, with feather-stuffed mattresses, quilts, and fur blankets, helped medieval lords and ladies stay warm while they slept. The bed was so large that usually there was little other furniture in the chamber—just a few stools and carved wooden chests for storage. Close to the chamber would be a garderobe (GAHR-drobe), a kind of indoor outhouse with a seat located over a chute that generally led to the moat. This was convenient, and more pleasant than using a chamber pot, but there was no toilet paper; hay was used instead.

Each floor of a castle typically had a place where water could be drawn from the well. Sometimes at the entrance to the great hall there was a stone basin for washing hands. A few castles had running water and a permanent bathhouse. But in most castles, when the lord or lady wanted to bathe, a wooden tub was set up in the chamber and filled with water heated in the fireplace. In good weather the tub might be placed in the garden and warmed by the sun. When great nobles traveled, they took along their bathtubs—and their beds and most of their other furniture—so that wherever they were, they could enjoy all the comforts of home.

A lady greets visitors in her solar, or sitting room. This painting from a French manuscript of the 1400s shows a luxurious room with a tiled floor, beautifully decorated walls, and a glass window with shutters.

A sixteenth-century bed in a German castle. This is a bit more elaborate than the beds used by nobles of the High Middle Ages. Their beds were just as high off the ground, however, and they were usually enclosed by curtains made of heavy and expensive cloth.

one end. Later the lord and lady's chamber was often a room above the hall or on an upper floor of one of the castle towers. Sometimes the lord and lady had separate chambers. In the largest castles they might also have one or more sitting rooms, called solars.

The castle's residents ate their meals together in the great hall, so a kitchen building was usually close by. Food was stored in or near the hall and on the ground floors of towers. A well and several cisterns, which caught rainwater, supplied water to the castle. For fresh vegetables, herbs, and fruit, a kitchen garden and small orchard were sometimes located within the curtain wall.

All European castles had chapels. Sometimes a castle chapel was a small room tucked into a tower; sometimes it was as big as a regular church. Later castles often had more than one chapel—a private one for the lord and his family and a larger one for the other residents. Services were generally held in the chapel every day, and many lords required everyone in their household to attend these services at least once a week.

Since the castle's function was mainly military, within the walls there were usually barracks for soldiers. (At some castles, though, soldiers slept in the great hall or near their guardposts.)

A castle kitchen of the High Middle Ages looked much like this reconstruction in Kreuzenstein Castle in Austria.

A stable was located near the barracks. In addition to the knights' warhorses, the stable also housed saddle horses and packhorses. A blacksmith worked at a forge near the stable, making horseshoes and other necessities.

Horses were not the only animals within the castle walls. Cats ran about freely, protecting stored food from mice and rats. Hunting hounds had their kennels, and a lord's favorite dogs might follow him wherever he went in the castle. Many ladies had pet lapdogs. Falconry (hunting with the help of birds of prey) was a favorite sport with nobles all over Europe, so a mews where hawks and falcons were kept was also a common feature of castles.

Although the castle was a self-contained community in many ways, few castles stood in isolation for long. Many were built to command important towns in the first place. Others were not far from country villages. Numerous castles overlooked major waterways, river crossings, roads, or mountain passes. Wherever the castle stood, it often attracted farmers, merchants, and craftspeople into its shadow, offering them protection and a market for their goods. In this way many towns and cities—for example, Edinburgh, Scotland—grew up around castles.

3

THE CASTLE COMMUNITY

A king or great noble held many castles, and during the course of a year he might visit several of them. In the twelfth and thirteenth centuries it was common for a lord to move on to a different location every month, or even every two weeks. Each castle generally had a "skeleton crew" of soldiers and servants who remained there all the time. Most of the household, however, traveled with the lord from place to place. A household of eight to thirty-five servants was typical at this time. These servants filled a variety of roles, but the most important task was to protect the lord, his family, and his valuables.

The group of knights and other military personnel who attended a lord were called his mesnie (may-NEE). Many members of the mesnie were permanent parts of the lord's household, although in England only the king had a regular bodyguard. Some of the mesnie were vassals on temporary military duty. Others were errants (AIR-unts), landless knights who often took service with a lord until they were able to become established landowners themselves. Many of a lord's knights served in nonmilitary positions when they were not needed to fight.

During the fourteenth century nobles became more settled, moving around much less than earlier. When they did travel, they took with them a small "riding household." This was separate from the main household, which was growing quite large. Most nobles now employed between thirty and seventy servants. The greatest lords, however, might have hundreds.

GUESTS OF THE CASTLE

In addition to the lord, his family, and his household, a castle frequently housed guests—the lord's vassals, his allies, his overlord or messengers from his overlord, relatives, and traveling churchmen among them. The lord and lady often raised and educated children from other noble families. After a battle or tournament, castle residents could also include nobles and knights being held for ransom. In the wake of war a lord often took hostages, usually family members of his enemy. He might hold these hostages in his castles for months or even years, as a guarantee that the hostages' families would keep peace with him, or because they had not paid the ransom. Such noble prisoners were usually kept under close guard but were well treated.

 A castle's lord and lady and their son are accompanied on an outing by ladies-in-waiting and other servants. This scene is from a famous series of tapestries known as the Unicorn Tapestries. They were woven around the year 1500 in what is now Belgium.

SERVANTS WHO SPECIALIZED

The highest-ranking servant was the steward, or seneschal (SEN-uh-shul). His duty was to generally oversee the household and keep everything running smoothly. He was empowered to make many decisions on behalf of the lord. He also supervised the lord's manors, the farmland that produced most of the lord's wealth. (By the 1200s the lord often hired a second steward, usually a knight, for this duty.) In addition, the steward might be the household's treasurer, although large establishments usually required a separate treasurer to keep track of expenses.

Another extremely important servant was the cook, who was highly paid for his specialized skills. He often supervised a very large staff. Some households also employed a kitchen clerk to handle and record food expenses. But it was the cook, or sometimes the steward, who made the decisions about what food to buy and prepare.

Large households needed a servant to keep order in the great hall, where everyone in the castle ate together. In the king of England's household this well-paid servant was the hall marshal; in the halls of great nobles a chief gentleman-usher often filled this job. His tasks included making sure that diners were seated according to their rank, overseeing the waiters, and, when necessary, breaking up fistfights during the meal.

The stable marshal was in charge of everything to do with the stableyard. He supervised huntsmen and the servants who cared for the lord's horses, hounds, and falcons. He also made sure that carts were in good repair, that saddles and other gear were well taken care of, and that the castle was always supplied with plenty of feed for the horses.

Every noble household employed at least one chaplain, a priest who was in charge of the castle's chapel and worship services. The chaplain oversaw the rest of the chapel staff, which could include other priests, caretakers for the chapel's valuable items, and perhaps a few singers. Occasionally chaplains also fulfilled the roles of steward and treasurer. Since chaplains and most other priests in noble households were well educated, they could act as secretaries and accountants as well.

Another specialized servant was the wardrober, who took care of the lord's costly clothes, jewels, and the like. Because he handled so many valuables and was well trusted, he might also act as the lord's treasurer. An almoner was a servant with different financial responsibilities: he distributed the lord's charitable donations to the poor.

Most lords kept a barber on hand—during the Middle Ages barbers not only cut hair and gave shaves but also performed dentistry and minor surgery. Some noble households included a physician or apothecary (a person who made medicines); others called in these medical specialists only when needed.

JACKS (AND JILLS) OF ALL TRADES

Many servants had general functions: the same man might wait at table, deliver messages, make purchases at local markets, and take care of other matters as needed. Some servants were craftspeople part of the time, making candles, soap, and the like.

The lord's most trusted servants tended to be his personal attendants. These were frequently lower-ranking noblemen, and they might do anything from helping the lord dress to going on diplomatic missions for him. In fact, a number of the chief servants

Servants dye cloth in a castle workshop.

in a castle could be of noble birth. In France and Italy, many of the lord's attendants and upper servants were his own cousins and other relatives.

Even many non-nobles were ranked as gentlemen, the servants who did the least physical labor. Lower in status were the valets. They often performed skilled jobs and had a great deal of responsibility. Valets' duties could include anything from assisting the stable marshal to making the lord's bed to slaughtering livestock. The lowest-ranking servants, grooms, had the hardest and dirtiest tasks, such as scrubbing pots and cleaning out stables. Valets and grooms typically came from peasant families in the villages near the castle.

In the Middle Ages, nearly all servants were male, and most of them were unmarried. If a servant was married, his wife and children usually did not live at the castle with him. An upper servant's wife, however, might become an attendant or lady-in-waiting to the lord's wife.

Occasionally a steward's or clerk's widow might take over his job. Otherwise, the only female servants in a castle were laundresses, caregivers for the lord's children, and the lady's personal attendants. Except for those who did the humblest jobs of the lady's chamber, these attendants, like the lord's, tended to be from noble families. Most were girls and young unmarried women. In addition, some of the lady's attendants were young boys, who ran light errands for her. Boys also worked in the kitchen and the bakery and did such chores as dusting.

For the most part, castle servants seem to have been contented with their lot. It was not unusual for a servant to be employed in the same household for twenty years or more, sometimes rising from groom to valet and even to gentleman. Nobles' servants enjoyed a fairly high standard of living, for in addition to their salaries, they received tips, rewards, and holiday bonuses. The lord also gave them free clothing, food, and shelter. The highest-ranking servants might even have their own rooms, and a number of servants had servants of their own.

4

A LORD'S DUTIES

A great lord's life centered around land. His manors supplied his household with wool, eggs, milk, grain, meat, and other farm products to use or sell. The people living on his land paid him rents and various taxes, tolls, fines, and fees. Land was wealth, and landownership made the lord powerful. The more land a lord held, the more vassals and other followers he could command. There were French lords—the dukes of Normandy and Aquitaine, the counts of Anjou and Champagne—whose holdings were so large that they rivaled kings.

Although lords received their fiefs from the king, they felt very strongly that the land they held belonged to them. Custom supported this, and usually when a lord died, his holdings passed to one or more of his sons. If he had no sons, in most areas a daughter could inherit. Whatever the arrangement, the important thing was to keep the land in the family.

Lords were willing to go to great lengths to keep and increase the lands they held. They sought favor with their overlord in the hope that he would grant them additional fiefs. They made marriages and alliances that brought new territory into their hands. Sometimes they used the legal system to prove that they

Planting the fields surrounding a French castle, from a manuscript of the early 1400s. One of the gentlemen strolling outside the castle wall may be the lord himself.

were the rightful owners of lands held by someone else. All too often, they turned to force.

FIGHTING FOR LORD AND LAND

Warfare was a fact of life, even a way of life, for knights and nobles. Part of a noble's obligation to his overlord was to fight for him. War could arise at any time, but in much of medieval Europe there was a traditional season for battles. This fighting season began after the Feast of Saint John (June 24) and continued for forty days, the amount of time that vassals were required to bear arms for their lords. Conflicts often lasted longer, of course, but generally no fighting was done in the winter.

Not only did lords fight each other, but a single lord's vassals frequently fought among themselves. Then the lord might feel the need to step in to stop this bloody quarreling in his territories. For example, in the 1170s the lords of southern France were violent rivals for control of the region. Count Richard of Poitou (who later became England's King Richard the Lion-Hearted) went to war to put an end to their feuding and to bring the territories firmly under his control. His actions were so brutal that the quarrelsome lords of southern France at last united—to resist Richard.

In fact, vassals often rebelled against their lords, in spite of their vows of loyalty. Nobles were very protective and proud of their rights. If they felt that their lord was limiting their power too much or making too many demands on them, they were usually

A fourteenth-century battle between the French and English in the Hundred Years' War. To the left sits the king of France, surrounded by the commanders of his army.

quick to rise against him. When a vassal saw the opportunity to gain more land and power, it was easy for him to find reasons for rebellion.

WARRIORS FOR GOD

Another kind of medieval warfare occurred for very different reasons. The Christian faith had a powerful effect on medieval European society. The Church taught that all people were basically sinful, but that acts of penance could earn forgiveness for sin. One of the most powerful acts of penance was going on a pilgrimage, and the greatest pilgrimage was to Jerusalem, the scene of several important events in the life of Jesus.

Christian Europe also had a long-standing rivalry with the Muslim world. In 1095 the pope, head of the Christian church in western Europe, sent out a call for knights to go to Jerusalem to take the holy city from its Muslim rulers. This was the beginning of the First Crusade, a pilgrimage and at the same time a war fought for God.

The crusaders faced great difficulties and danger—it was a long, hard journey just to get to the Middle East. They knew they would be away from home for between one and three years, and they worried about how their families and lands would fare in their absence. Crusading was also extremely expensive, costing a knight up to three times his usual annual income. Nevertheless, numerous lords joined the First Crusade with great enthusiasm. The idea of winning forgiveness from sin (and a place in heaven) by going to war—the thing they had been trained to do since childhood—was very powerful. Crusading quickly became one of the things expected of the perfect knight.

The Crusades continued to occur on and off throughout the twelfth and thirteenth centuries. Many knights never returned to

Knights Hospitaller defend their kingdom against a Muslim army.

Europe—in addition to those who were killed in battle, great numbers died of thirst, starvation, or disease. Some lords and their followers settled in the Holy Land, for the crusaders established several realms of their own, the most important being the Kingdom of Jerusalem. Other men stayed to become Knights Templar or Knights Hospitaller, members of religious military groups sworn to defend the Holy Land and assist pilgrims there. The Templars and the Hospitallers built some of the Middle Ages' greatest castles. Many of these can still be seen in the Middle East today.

CHAUCER'S KNIGHT

Geoffrey Chaucer, who lived from about 1340 to 1400, was one of the greatest writers in English literature. His most famous book is *The Canterbury Tales*, in which a group of people on a pilgrimage to the shrine of Saint Thomas à Becket, in Canterbury, entertain one another by telling stories. One of the pilgrims is a knight, accompanied by his son, a squire. Chaucer's knight has taken part in a number of crusades, including wars against the Muslims of Spain and non-Christian peoples of northern Europe (these wars were also thought of as crusades). Crusading had become part of the knightly ideal, and Chaucer wanted his character to be a model of knighthood. The squire, on the other hand, has had no real battle experience yet but is a fashionable master of courtly skills. Here, in a modern English adaptation, is Chaucer's description of the knight and his son:

A knight there was—and that a worthy man—
That from the time that he first began
To ride to battle, he loved chivalry,
Truth and honor, freedom and courtesy.
Full worthy was he in his lord's war,
And thereto had he ridden, no man so far,
In both Christendom and in heathen places.
He was ever honored for his worthiness.
When Alexandria was won, he was there.
At table he had the place of honor
Full often for his deeds in Prussia.

The Squire

In Lithuania had he fought, and in Russia—
More than any man of his degree.
In Granada also at the siege was he. . . .

. . .

His fame was the kind most highly prized,
And brave as he was, he was also wise.
Like a maiden, his bearing was meek,
And no rudeness did he ever speak
To anyone in any rank of life.
He was a true, perfect, noble knight.

. . .

With him there was his son, a young squire,
A lover and a lively bachelor
With curling hair about his shoulders.
He was twenty years old, I guess, no older.
Of his stature he was of average length,
And wonderfully agile, with great strength.

. . .

He was singing or whistling all the day—
He was as fresh as is the month of May.
Short was his gown, with sleeves long and wide.
Well could he sit on horse and beautifully ride.
He could make tunes, with words to fit them right,
Joust, and also dance, and well draw and write.

The Knight

PEACEFUL PASTIMES

When a lord was not at war, there was still plenty for him to do. He had his lands to look after, and he had his various peacetime duties to his overlord. In addition he usually had responsibilities in the justice system.

In England the most serious crimes were tried only by the king's court, while in France and Germany they were tried by kings and also by great lords. These crimes included treason, making false money, theft, kidnapping, arson, and murder and other violent

A nobleman and his friends take a break from their hunting to have a grand meal outdoors.

offenses. Accused criminals were sometimes briefly held in a castle tower or storage area while they awaited trial, but criminals were rarely sentenced, as we might think, to be thrown into dungeons. During most of the Middle Ages, people convicted in the high courts were usually either executed or maimed. For example, a thief might be punished by having his hand cut off.

Each lord administered his own court to handle the less serious and nonviolent crimes that occurred on his lands. Usually the lord's steward presided over the court for him. Convicted criminals were charged fines, which were paid to the lord. In fact, such fines often made up a good portion of a lord's income.

Another source of income and prestige for a lord was to hold a post in the king's government. (Kings paid handsome salaries to their officials and often gave them additional rewards.) English nobles sometimes went to great lengths to get themselves or their friends appointed as sheriffs, the officers in charge of individual shires, or counties. Chancellor, chamberlain, treasurer, and constable were some of the other royal posts a lord could fill in England. Knights and lesser lords in France held office as viscounts (similar to English sheriffs), seneschals, and overseers of trade fairs, among other things.

When a lord had some free time, a favorite activity was hunting. Most lords set aside large portions of their land as game preserves. Knights and nobles rode on horseback when they hunted, using dogs and falcons to help them bring down game. Hunting was good exercise, and it supplied the household with fresh meat. Since it required excellent riding skills, it also helped keep knights in shape for battle.

5

A LADY'S DAYS

In theory, only men took part in the feudal relationship between lord and vassal. Most medieval priests, lawmakers, and other thinkers believed that women were too weak, unintelligent, and prone to sin to be trusted in positions of power. Actually, though, it was common for noblewomen to hold fiefs—sometimes very large and important ones.

Not only could a daughter inherit land, but a widow kept from one-third to one-half of her dead husband's property. Since warfare and other dangerous activities played a major part in the lives of medieval men, their death rate was very high. One study has shown that between 1350 and 1500, 25 percent of English noblemen never reached the age of forty. The result was that many women were widowed and many men had no living sons to inherit their lands.

Like a male holder of a fief, an heiress or widow pledged loyalty and support to her overlord, and she generally fulfilled the same duties as a male vassal. However, she was not expected—or trained—to provide military service. If she married or remarried, this responsibility fell on her husband. For this reason, the overlord of a noble heiress or widow had a great deal of control over whom she married. If she refused to marry the man her lord picked for

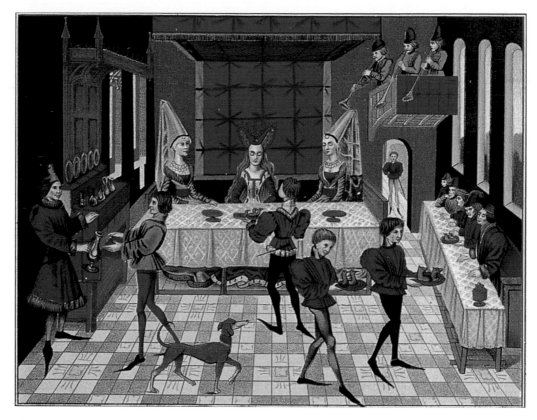

Three noblewomen sit at the head table during a feast. From a balcony above them, minstrels entertain with music. The women's elaborate headdresses were popular during the fifteenth century, especially in France.

her, if she wished to marry someone of her own choice, or if she wanted to remain unmarried (though this was rare), she was required to pay the lord a large fee.

A woman who held a fief could have many vassals of her own. She presided over the justice system on her lands and performed other duties expected of a lord. Sometimes her husband took on authority over her territory, but it seems that in most places the heiress or widow was usually able to exercise her full rights to rule.

ELEANOR OF AQUITAINE

One of medieval Europe's most notable and remarkable women was Eleanor of Aquitaine. In 1137, at the age of fifteen, she inherited her father's vast landholdings in southern France. A few months later she was married to the seventeen-year-old son of the king of France. Shortly after the marriage the king died, and Eleanor was crowned queen of France beside her husband, the new King Louis VII. For several years Eleanor had great influence over Louis, advising him on matters of statecraft and war.

In 1145 Louis announced that he would undertake a crusade to the Holy Land, where the crusader kingdoms established after the First Crusade were under threat. The Second Crusade departed France in the summer of 1147. Eleanor and many other noblewomen—some of them dressed and armed like men—were among the warrior-pilgrims. Indeed, Eleanor's great wealth and numerous vassals made the crusade possible.

The expedition was, however, a disaster. Many men were lost to hardships and ambushes on the way to the Holy Land. The crusaders won no new territory, and the existing crusader kingdoms were as insecure as ever. And during the course of the crusade, Eleanor determined to end her marriage to Louis. The king, however, would not hear of it. After celebrating Easter 1149 in Jerusalem, they finally returned to France.

Soon afterward, Eleanor gave birth to a daughter, their second. Since Eleanor had not given Louis a son and heir during fifteen years of marriage, he seems to have decided that divorcing her was now his best course. With the consent of the Church, the pair were separated in 1152. Louis kept their two daughters, but Eleanor kept her lands, to which she returned.

Two months later Eleanor married Henry, Duke of Normandy and Count of Anjou. She had met him the year before, at court in Paris, when he was eighteen and a new-made knight. The joining of their lands made the pair a formidable force. In 1154 Henry, grandson of Henry I, became king of England. This began a long period of rivalry between the kings of England and France.

Eleanor and Henry had five sons and three daughters. Henry was a busy and restless king, frequently off to war or making the rounds of his French landholdings. When he was away, Eleanor ruled England in his place. By 1170, however, she had grown tired of England and of Henry's wandering ways. She returned to her ancestral lands, to the city of Poitiers. Here she established her own court, where she hosted the best poets and musicians in France. This was a splendid time, but it did not last long. In 1173 Henry's three oldest sons rebelled against him, and Eleanor supported their cause. After Henry quashed the rebellion, he took Eleanor back to England and confined her to one of his castles. She was not released until 1185. Four years later Henry died, and his son Richard (the Lion-Hearted) succeeded him as king.

Richard was Eleanor's favorite son, and she now returned to a place of honor and power. Once more Eleanor ruled as Queen of England, for Richard spent nearly all his reign in France or on crusade (and for two years after the Third Crusade, he was held prisoner in Germany by the Holy Roman Emperor). When Richard died in 1199, his brother John became king. Eleanor assisted this son, too, in establishing his rule. She went on diplomatic missions for him and was even besieged by his enemies in the French castle of Mirebeau. But after this Eleanor retired from public life. She returned to her beloved Poitiers, and there she died in 1204, at the age of eighty-two. She had lived a long and remarkable life.

WIVES AND MOTHERS

A noblewoman who did not hold fiefs of her own still had a very important position. She assisted her husband in many ways, and she was generally in charge of the household. She oversaw all of the servants and might even supervise the management of the lord's manors. The lady often had responsibility for the family finances and for making payments to retainers, employees, charities, and so on. She greeted and entertained important guests for her husband, and sometimes she even fulfilled his official duties, such as holding court.

In the feudal point of view, however, the lady's most important function was to provide the lord with sons who could inherit his fiefs. Noblewomen often had ten or more children. But even among nobles, many mothers died in childbirth because medieval medical knowledge was very limited. Babies, too, frequently died during or soon after birth. Because of these dangers, during a lady's pregnancy the noble family's chaplain said special prayers for both her and her unborn child. The lord and lady themselves were likely to pray to various saints for a safe birth and might also make a pilgrimage to a saint's shrine.

Even if a lady lived through childbirth, her babies were cared for largely by servants. The medieval noblewoman did not breast-feed her child but, according to the custom of the time, hired a wet nurse to do this.* However, as her children grew older, the lady did

*This custom may have developed because people believed that if a nursing mother became pregnant, her milk would no longer be good for the baby she was breastfeeding. Noblewomen were expected to bear as many children as possible, and so their frequent pregnancies prevented them from being able to nurse their own babies, according to the beliefs of the time.

Surrounded by relatives, a mother cradles her newborn in her arms.

play a role in their education. She also took part in the training of other children in the household, usually children of her husband's vassals or allies.

Altogether, a lady's days were very full. In her leisure time she enjoyed many of the same activities as the lord, such as playing chess and hunting with falcons. She also did fine embroidery and weaving. A favorite pastime was reading. In fact, medieval noblewomen tended to read a great deal more than their husbands did. Ladies read the Psalms and other religious works, but romances were especially popular. These medieval romances were long poems that often told stories of the knights and ladies of King Arthur's court. The tales were full of love, magic, and heroic deeds. They are still enjoyed by many people today.

A lady seated at an elaborate reading desk enjoys her book.

LADIES AT WAR

The lord of a castle was often away. In his absence the lady ruled his lands—and protected them if necessary. If the lord died, leaving his lands to his son, it often happened that the heir was still a child. Then, in most places, the boy's mother became his guardian until he was an adult. This too put the lady in the position of having to rule and protect the land.

There are a number of accounts of noble wives, mothers, widows, and heiresses defending castles. In 1341 while the countess of Brittany's husband was away, one of their castles came under attack. The countess was there and organized the defense. She assigned the castle's women and children to tear out the courtyard's paving stones and take them to the soldiers on the wall, who dropped the stones down on the attackers. The countess even led out an army to chase off the enemy. Although it was not common, throughout the Middle Ages there were other noblewomen who, when necessary, personally fought off invaders, led armies, recruited soldiers, and even ordered the building of castles.

The medieval lady did not always stay home at the castle. Often she went along with the lord on his travels. A number of noble-women even accompanied their husbands on the Crusades. There are some records of women fighting in battles in the Middle East, but it is hard to tell if any of them were ladies; many other women also went on the Crusades. Noblewomen traveled without their husbands, too, touring the family's different castles and manors, visiting the overlord's court, going on pilgrimage, and the like. These ladies were not the timid princesses of the average fairy tale!

6

A NOBLE
UPBRINGING

The babies of nobles were always born at home, usually with the help of one or more midwives. Newborns were given very tender care. They were bathed in lukewarm water at least once a day; gently rubbed with oil; wrapped in soft, warm swaddling clothes; kept away from strong light; and picked up whenever they cried. Many noble infants had cradles in which they could be rocked. In some castles babies had their own room, opening off the mother's chamber, heated by a special stove so that they would not catch cold.

In normal circumstances, a baby was baptized, or brought into the Christian faith, when it was a week old. The child also received its name at this time. During the High Middle Ages noble babies were usually named after a relative, but sometimes they were named after a saint, or occasionally after a legendary hero.

A lord and lady's children were closely attended as they grew. When they began to walk, the wet nurse or parents made sure that there was a bench nearby to which they could hold on. Because toddlers fell down a lot, they were given padded bonnets to protect their heads. By the thirteenth century many noble children had

A noble family of fifteenth-century France. The children wear miniature versions of adult clothing. They appear to be listening closely to their father's advice.

walkers, little chairs with wheels on the legs. Medieval writers instructed parents and wet nurses to use gentleness, encouragement, and praise with toddlers as they learned to walk and talk.

Up till the age of three, both boys and girls were cared for by their mothers and wet nurses. Then a boy's nurse might be replaced by a tutor, and at the age of four he might start learning to ride horses. A girl's nurse often continued to care for her and serve her long after breastfeeding was done with. Until the children were about seven, their mother had the main responsibility for teaching them basic Christian beliefs, important prayers, and some of the Psalms.

BLIND MAN'S BUFF

In medieval Europe, people of all ages and all social ranks enjoyed playing games. One of the oldest and most popular games was blind man's buff. It is still fun to play today. To start, select one player to be It, and cover his or her eyes. Any piece of cloth can make a good blindfold, but to give a more medieval flavor to the game, use a hood or an animal mask. In any case, It should not be able to see anything at all.

The other players make a circle around It, and one of them gently turns It around a few times. Then the players, one at a time, run to the center of the circle and lightly "buffet," or tap, It. It tries to catch these players before they can return to their places. When a player is caught, It must identify him or her— without being able to see, of course! The first person whom It names correctly now becomes It, and the game starts all over again!

During this part of childhood there was also lots of time to play. Toys included rattles, whistles, drums, blocks, balls, tops, see-saws, miniature windmills, small wooden boats, clay animals, hobby horses, rocking horses, and marionettes. Noble girls might have several dolls, and boys had wooden swords and shields. Sometimes children got permission to play with things that belonged to their parents—their mother's jewelry, for example. Boys and girls played imaginatively, too, both on their own and in groups. They also enjoyed many games, in which adults often joined.

At about the age of seven, girls and boys were separated. Training for the roles they would play as adults now began in earnest.

THE FUTURE KNIGHT

After age seven, the oldest son was generally educated at home under the supervision of his father, since he would one day inherit his father's position and property. By the age of nine, a younger son was usually sent to the castle of another noble—an uncle, a friend of his father's, or his father's overlord. There he became a page, serving his foster father's knights and learning from them. If a noble family had many sons, one or two of them might be sent to a monastery or, a little later, to a university. These sons would be educated for careers in the church, in law, or in government administration.

Most noble boys were destined to become knights. Until the twelfth century, it was unusual for them to learn how to read. Their education focused on archery, horsemanship, and other warrior skills.

Even recreation educated them for the future. Learning to play chess taught them to think strategically. Active games, including various ball games, helped them learn to react quickly, to think on their feet, and to handle themselves in the midst of action. Many of these games were played together by a large group of boys being trained at the castle, so the future knights also learned about teamwork.

Much of a page's training involved simply observing the life of his foster father's court, learning from the examples of the adults around him. The behavior of the knights and ladies was reinforced by songs and stories that taught the ideals of chivalry. A page learned that the perfect knight was brave, loyal, generous, and honorable. As a Christian warrior, he was expected to be just and truthful, modest and merciful. He should use his strength and skill to protect the Church and all those who were weaker than he. Beginning in the twelfth century, the ideal knight was also what we might call a perfect gentleman. He was courteous and well mannered, he respected all noblewomen, and he faithfully served his chosen lady. His speech was gracious. He should be able to sing, play at least one musical instrument, and dance. He might even learn to read and write—not only in his own language, but also in Latin, and perhaps in one or more foreign languages.

At about age twelve knightly training became intense. Swordsmanship, wrestling, attacking targets while on horseback, and hunting were skills that had to be mastered now. At the age of fifteen the page generally became a squire. He served one particular knight, caring for his horse and armor, waiting on him at table, and following him to war. Two to four years later, the squire was at last ready to become a knight himself.

 Two boys learn the art of falconry, hunting with the help of trained hawks or falcons.

The young man could be knighted by his foster father, his own father, his father's overlord, or the knight who had trained him. Sometimes all the squires in a household were knighted together by the lord of the castle. The knighting could occur on a special occasion or before an upcoming battle. Some young men were knighted after a battle, right on the battlefield, in recognition of their achievements.

Initiation into knighthood was usually a splendid event. The ceremonies, as they took shape in the twelfth century, began with a bath to cleanse the body. Then the knight-to-be sat up through the night in the castle chapel, praying to purify his soul. In the morning he attended a religious service, followed by breakfast with friends and family. Then he dressed in a new set of garments, all white, and was led to the place of the knighting. His father and other knights helped him into his armor and presented him with a sword that had been blessed by a priest. The young man kissed the hilt of the sword. At last the man who was knighting him gave him the accolade, the kiss or blow on the cheek that officially made the squire a knight. (One medieval writer explained that the blow—which often knocked the young man to the ground—was supposed to help the new knight remember the importance of keeping his vows.) Once the ceremony was over, it was time for feasting and perhaps even a tournament, where the new knight could show off his prowess.

FROM CHILD TO BRIDE

Like their knightly brothers, most noble girls were also carefully trained. They were usually taught at home by their mothers, often with the help of tutors or governesses. Some girls went to convents for their education (a number of these girls later became nuns), and some went to the court of another noble. Wherever a girl was educated, training in good manners, hospitality, and household management was of high importance. Many of these things were learned by observing the lady of the castle and following her example.

It was also very common for the daughters of lords to learn to read and, often, to write. Some mastered more than one language. Many studied arithmetic and became familiar with land laws in preparation for their future. Like their brothers, they were taught to ride, to train and hunt with falcons, and to play chess. The ideal lady also knew how to embroider and weave, sing and dance, play a musical instrument, and tell stories. Some basic medical knowledge—along the lines of first aid—was also considered useful for the future wife of a knight.

As a noble girl was being educated, plans were already under way for her marriage. In the Middle Ages, nearly all marriages were arranged by the families of the bride and groom. Although the Church decreed that the couple had to consent to the marriage, in practice they often had no say in the matter. Young women and men of the peasantry had the most freedom of choice. Nobles had the least, since their marriages could have a huge impact on landholding and politics. Marriage was a way to make alliances and to gain additional lands. It had nothing to do with love—frequently the bride and groom did not even meet until the wedding.

According to the law, a girl had to be at least twelve to get married, and a boy had to be fourteen. Most noble families did stay well within these guidelines: It was common for men to be in their twenties when they married, and brides were usually between the ages of fourteen and eighteen. But among royalty and the very

A noble Italian bride and groom of the early 1400s are congratulated by their families.

highest nobles, couples were often engaged when they were babies or toddlers. Sometimes young children actually got married. For example, in 1160 the five-year-old heir of the king of England was married to the three-year-old daughter of the king of France.

Even though a noble marriage rarely started with love, love often grew. One lord, still grieving over his wife many years after her death, wrote about how he had composed songs and poems for her while she was alive. Most couples at least shared a bond of common purpose as they strove together to hold and rule their land and pass it on to the next generation.

7

FESTIVITIES, TOURNAMENTS, AND TROUBADOURS

Weddings, knightings, baptisms—these were some of the most festive occasions in the medieval castle. Splendid celebrations occurred for holidays, too. The most important holidays were Christmas and Easter, which honored Christ's birth and his rising from the dead. Kings and great lords often held a Christmas court and an Easter court, their major gatherings of the year. Along with religious services, feasting, and entertainment, judgments were passed, high councils met, and lords and vassals renewed their pledges.

For Christmas in many places the castle was decorated with holly and ivy, and a huge Yule log burned in the great hall's fireplace. The lord presented gifts of new clothing to all in his household. Kings often gave their knights and retainers lavish presents, such as saddle horses, jewels, gold and silver cups, and costly garments. The Christmas festivities lasted a full twelve days, from December 25 to January 6. Songs, dances, games, and feasting were part of the celebration for young and old, noble and servant alike.

Lords and ladies circle around in a stately dance. Dancing was an enjoyable part of many medieval feasts and celebrations.

In February or March, forty-six days before Easter, the season of Lent began. During this serious time of prayer and penance, the cross in the castle chapel was covered with a shroud, a piece of cloth like the kind used to wrap a dead body. On the Friday preceding

Easter, the cross was buried or hidden in a special place in the chapel. The next night every candle and fire in the castle was put out. Then, with great ceremony, a new fire was kindled and a special Easter candle was lit. In the chapel the priests and others held an all-night vigil. When Easter morning dawned, they brought out the cross and placed it upon the altar. A solemn and joyful service was held, followed by a bountiful feast.

Advent (several weeks before Christmas) and Lent were seasons when people were expected to put aside many of their worldly concerns and focus their thoughts on religion. During these times, too, the Church declared the Truce of God, when no one should commit any kind of violence. In particular, lords were expected not to engage in warfare during the Truce of God. Many tried to keep the peace, but few were successful on a regular basis.

KNIGHTLY CONTESTS

Shortly after Easter the season of tournaments began. These contests among knights, organized by great lords, were a sport, a form of entertainment, and practice for battle. When a tournament was proclaimed, hundreds of knights and their squires came from far and wide to attend. Spectators, too, flocked to the gathering. Tents were set up on open land, and the inns of the nearest town overflowed.

A festival atmosphere surrounded tournaments. They attracted horse dealers, armor makers, food sellers, and a variety of other merchants. Storytellers, minstrels, and acrobats were among the performers who found enthusiastic audiences. Ladies came dressed in their finest, ready to cheer on their favorite knights. There were stone-throwing contests, wrestling matches, and dice games. There

FOOD FIT FOR A KING

Nobles and their households ate well. Unlike most peasants, castle residents were usually able to eat meat almost every day. Beef and mutton were the most commonly eaten red meats, but veal, lamb, and pork were also popular. Chicken was prepared in a variety of ways and was greatly enjoyed. Game animals frequently graced noble tables: deer, wild boar, and duck, as well as geese, pigeons, herons, and other birds.

During Advent and Lent, and on Wednesdays, Fridays, and Saturdays all year round, devout medieval Christians did not eat meat. Fish (which was not considered meat by the Church) was consumed instead. Noble households enjoyed an enormous variety of seafood, but among the favorites were salmon, trout, herring, lobster, crab, and oysters.

On a holiday or other special occasion, meals became elaborate feasts with numerous courses. In addition to the more common meats, there were delicacies such as roast swan or peacock. Exotic imported fruits—oranges, lemons, dates, figs— were used as ingredients in special recipes. Rich sauces were seasoned with cinnamon, ginger, pepper, and other expensive spices from the East. Edible flowers decorated cakes and tarts. Sometimes the cook concocted spectacular food sculptures, often made of marzipan. You can make this delicious confection yourself.

To make marzipan, you will need:

1 pound blanched almonds
a little ice water
2 egg whites
1⅓ cup confectioner's sugar
¼ cup orange juice or lemon juice
Optional: a couple pinches of cinnamon, cloves, and/or ginger
For decoration: food coloring (medieval people used edible plants—parsley, violets, and saffron, for example—to get their food dyes, but you can buy yours at the supermarket)

Grind the almonds—the medieval way is to use a mortar and pestle, but you could use a blender or food processor. Every so often add a bit of ice water to the almonds so that they do not become too oily. You should end up with a thick paste.

Put the egg whites into a large bowl and beat them until they form peaks. Beat in the confectioner's sugar a little at a time.

Put the almond paste into the bowl, too, and add the spices if you want to. Wet your fingers with the juice and knead the mixture for ten minutes. Whenever it feels too sticky, add a bit more juice.

Now you have marzipan. Divide it into as many portions as you have colors. Wrap each portion separately (in waxed paper, aluminum foil, or plastic wrap) and put it into the refrigerator for a day or two.

When you are ready to work with the marzipan, let it warm to room temperature first. Take each portion one at a time. Squeeze a few drops of food coloring onto it, then knead it until the coloring is completely mixed in. (Wet your fingers with ice water if the marzipan is too sticky.) When you have colored all of the marzipan, you are ready to sculpt it into fruit or animal shapes or whatever you can imagine.

From a safe distance, a queen and her ladies-in-waiting watch a furiously fought tournament.

was dancing in the meadows and on town greens. Outside the tents and in the streets of the town, tables were set up for feasting by candlelight.

In the twelfth and thirteenth centuries, the actual tournament was a mock battle between two groups of knights on horseback. The groups assembled at opposite ends of a huge field. A signal was given, and the two sides charged toward each other. They fought almost as fiercely as if it were a real battle. When one band of horsemen retreated from the field in defeat, the other band chased after them, taking as many prisoners as they could. A captured knight was held for ransom. He had to give his horse and armor to his captor, or else pay him a large amount of money to get them back. Many errant knights made a living—and some made a fortune—by winning at tournaments.

In the fourteenth century these chaotic mock battles gave way to jousting. This was a form of mounted combat between two knights, who took their places at opposite ends of the field. Then, with lowered lances, they rode at each other as hard as they could, each trying to knock the other off his horse. These exciting contests lasted for days, because the winner of each joust then went up against other winners. At last every knight was defeated except one, the champion. He was sometimes rewarded with a prize in addition to the ransoms he had already collected.

In both tournaments and jousts, men were often killed or permanently injured. Kings and churchmen tried at various times to outlaw these violent contests. Nevertheless, they remained part of the knightly way of life throughout the Middle Ages.

THE LANGUAGE OF LOVE

Tournaments celebrated the military aspect of the noble life, but there was also an artistic side. The noble courts of the High Middle Ages were the homes of great poetry, music, and storytelling. Much of this art celebrated romantic love. In fact, this was the first time in Christian Europe that romantic love was considered a worthy subject for literature and song. And these odes to love were written not in Latin, the language of learning, but in the languages that people spoke every day.

The new love songs and love poems began in southern France with the troubadours, who were both poets and composers. The first known troubadour was William IX, Duke of Aquitaine. His granddaughter, Eleanor of Aquitaine, was a great supporter of troubadours and other poets. So was her daughter, Countess Marie of Champagne. Marie's grandson Thibaut, count of Champagne and king of Navarre, became one of medieval France's greatest poet-composers.

Throughout the twelfth and thirteenth centuries, troubadour songs were heard regularly in the castles of southern France. Sometimes they were performed by the poet, sometimes by another singer. Musicians playing instruments such as harp and vielle (a kind of early violin) might accompany the songs. Many of the poets and performers traveled from castle to castle. The

A lady plays a harp to entertain herself and her companions as they relax in a castle garden. This beautiful tapestry was woven in 1420 in Flanders (now part of Belgium).

A TROUBADOUR SONG

One of the troubadours who was especially popular at the court of Eleanor of Aquitaine was Bernart de Ventadorn. It was said that he was the son of a peasant, but that nevertheless God gave him a noble heart, wisdom, courtesy, and the art of composing good poetry and music. Here is a selection from his song "Non es meravelha s'eu chan" ("It is no wonder if I sing"):

It is no wonder if I sing
Better than any other man,
For my heart more to love is drawn,
And love's laws I excel at following.
Heart and body, senses and mind,
Strength and power—to love they are trained.
I am pulled toward love like a horse in rein,
And to nothing else can I attend.

When I see her, my feelings show in
My eyes, my face, my changing color—
So much do I tremble in fear,
As does the leaf against the wind.
I have no more sense than a baby,
For love has left me all undone,
And for a man so overcome,
A lady ought to show great mercy.

Good lady, I ask you for no more
Than that you take me as a servant.
For me it is reward sufficient
To have you as my ruling lord.
You see me ready at your command,
Heart honest, humble, gay, and courtly.
I trust you are not so fierce as to kill me
If I give myself into your hand.

nobles who enjoyed their songs also traveled widely, and soon troubadour-style love songs spread to Spain, Italy, northern France, England, and Germany.

A common theme in these songs was a man's love for a noble lady. Often the lady did not return his love. Nevertheless, the man praised her beauty, her sense, her courtesy, and other noble qualities. He swore to be her vassal and serve her faithfully all his life. Yet he still wished that she would give him some sign of her favor. This "courtly" love was an important theme in the popular romance tales of the Middle Ages, too—and it has not gone out of fashion yet.

8

CASTLE CRISES

lthough castles were the homes of the most privileged people of the Middle Ages, castle life was not always easy or entirely comfortable. Fleas and lice infested all medieval dwellings, including those of the nobles. People generally bathed only once a week, if that, and clothes were not washed often, either. With mainly candles for lighting and fireplaces for heating, castles tended to be rather dim and chilly. Castle residents had little privacy.

Diseases affected the rich and powerful just as much as the poor. Nobles were able to hire physicians, midwives, surgeons, and apothecaries, but often there was little these medical people could do. The workings of the human body and the causes of disease were poorly understood in medieval Europe. So even among the nobility, death was a frequent visitor.

Discomfort and disease were bad enough, but war was worse. Castles existed because of warfare, but this was also the greatest danger to them. A lord seeking to conquer territory focused his attacks on the castles guarding it, for whoever held the castles could hold the land.

Sometimes an attacker was able to storm a castle and overrun its defenses quickly. Traitors within the walls might help the enemy

The most feared disease of the Middle Ages was the Black Plague, which swept through Europe in several waves. It struck in village, city, and castle alike, and there was no cure. Queen Anne, wife of Richard II of England, died of the plague in 1394.

get in. More often, though, the attacker had to lay siege to the castle. With an army encamped outside the walls, the defenders were cut off from reinforcements and supplies. On the other hand, many castles had enough food stored to last a year or more. So long as the well did not dry up (as sometimes happened), the residents of such a castle were quite likely to outlast the enemy.

Attackers, however, tended not to wait passively for the defenders to surrender. A common technique was to tunnel beneath the castle walls. As soon as the tunnel was most of the way under the wall, it was allowed to collapse, and the section of wall on top collapsed with it.

If the castle was built on solid rock, so that tunneling was not an option, various siege engines, such as battering rams, catapults, and assault towers, could be used. Battering rams, used to break down walls and doors, worked best on smaller or older fortresses. Several types of catapults were employed to fling heavy stones and other missiles over the walls. Often they hurled flaming objects that set the castle buildings on fire. Assault towers were only effective if the attackers managed to fill in the castle's moat with dirt and stones. Then the tall wooden towers, full of soldiers, could be pushed right up to the walls.

If all else failed, the attackers could resort to trickery. Sometimes a small force would quietly climb the wall during the night, or get into the castle through a garderobe, garbage chute, or out-of-use well. Or the attackers might lure the castle guards out, only to chase them back in through the gatehouse. There were even times when a besieging force pretended to give up and march away. Then some of the knights would disguise themselves as merchants selling needed provisions. When they were allowed into the castle, they would seize the gatehouse and admit the rest of the army.

In spite of all these techniques, many castles survived sieges. A few were so well situated and formidable that they were never besieged at all. Numerous castles remain standing today, lasting monuments to the brave, courteous, creative lords and ladies of the Middle Ages.

A castle under siege. The attackers are trying to tunnel under the walls. They work beneath a rolling wooden shelter that barely protects them from the rocks, torches, and other missiles hurled down by the defenders in the tower.

THE CITY

1

URBAN EUROPE

In ancient Greece and Rome, city life was well established. The Romans in particular developed an urban lifestyle, which they carried with them to every part of their empire. Everywhere from Britain to North Africa to Asia Minor there were thriving Roman cities.

After the collapse of the Roman Empire in 476, numerous cities fell into decay. Constant warfare brought trade—the lifeblood of cities—almost to a halt. In northwest Europe especially, rural life became far more important as power was concentrated in the hands of large landowners. Local farming was the most important element of the economy. Most areas produced only what they needed; there was rarely a surplus of food or goods that could be traded.

The Roman cities that survived—for example, Paris (France) and Cologne (Germany)—were often those where a bishop had his headquarters. A bishop was a high-ranking Christian priest who oversaw religious affairs for a particular region; a bishop's church was called a cathedral. But for some time even a cathedral city might be composed of only sixty to eighty small houses, and most of the city's area might still be gardens, orchards, and pastures.

At first the situation was better for cities in what is now southern France, on the Mediterranean coast. Marseilles and other

In this scene from the legend of Saint Ursula by artist Hans Memling, the saint and her companions arrive at the German city of Cologne. Cologne Cathedral, which rises in the background here, was begun in 1248. The city had started its life as a Roman colony twelve hundred years before that.

towns continued to do business with the ports of the eastern Mediterranean. This trade, too, was interrupted when Muslim warriors swept through the Mediterranean world in the seventh and eighth centuries. Wherever they settled, these warriors brought along their religion, Islam. Soon ancient cities such as Alexandria (Egypt) and Córdoba (Spain) again flourished, this time under Muslim rule. The followers of Islam also established thriving new cities, including Cairo (Egypt) and Baghdad (Iraq). During this period the only really great Christian city was Constantinople (now Istanbul, Turkey), center of the wealthy Byzantine Empire.*

Slowly, however, cities were beginning to make a comeback in northwest Europe. The sixth and seventh centuries saw the spread of Christian monasteries, highly organized communities devoted to religious life. Craftspeople, merchants, and farmers were quick to gather around the monasteries. Some of these monastic centers eventually grew into true cities, for example Germany's "Monks' Town"—Munich.

Trade was reviving, and market centers were starting to flourish. One such center was Dorestad in what is today the Netherlands. By the ninth century Dorestad and similar places were wealthy enough to attract Viking raiders. Many coastal and riverside settlements suffered heavily from Viking attacks. However, towns also strengthened their fortifications as a result of the Viking raids, and many fortresses built as defenses against the Vikings soon grew into cities. The Vikings themselves founded a number of new cities, and not only in their Scandinavian homeland: for example, Dublin was one of many Irish cities established by the Vikings.

*The Byzantine Empire was the successor of the eastern half of the ancient Roman Empire. Its core was Asia Minor and Greece, and its culture was quite different from that of the rest of medieval Europe.

All of these upheavals had limited effect on northern Italy. Here, without interruption, city life continued to be of great importance. Milan, Florence, Pisa, Bologna, Verona, Padua, and Genoa had all been well-established urban communities since Roman times or even earlier. Rome itself, "the eternal city," maintained a special place in European culture, for its bishop, the pope, was the head of the Catholic Church of western Europe.

One major Italian city did not have its origin in the Roman Empire but actually arose during the Middle Ages. This was Venice, founded in 697 by the union of several communities built on

HOW BIG WAS A BIG CITY?

By modern standards, medieval cities had rather small populations. However, an average country village of the time had only from 150 to 250 residents. In comparison, the cities were very heavily populated indeed.

Here are western Europe's largest cities around the year 1250, ranked by approximate population:

80,000–100,000: Venice (Italy)
50,000 to 100,000: Genoa and Milan (Italy)
50,000: Paris (France); Bologna and Palermo (Italy)
40,000: Ghent (Flanders—now Belgium)
25,000: London (England); Marseilles, Toulouse, Lille, and Rouen (France); Florence and Naples (Italy)
10,000: York (England); Barcelona and Seville (Spain); Troyes and Montpellier (France); Cologne (Germany); and many others

marshy islands just off the northeast coast of Italy. Within a few centuries Venice was a great power in the Mediterranean, and by 1201 it was the trading capital of Europe.

In northern Europe, the High Middle Ages saw the founding of other major cities, such as Belfast (Ireland), Amsterdam (Netherlands), Copenhagen (Denmark), and Berlin (Germany). Older cities continued to thrive and grow, making urban life a vital part of medieval culture.

2

WHO RAN
THE CITIES?

𝕿here was no one standard type of government for medieval cities. Many were directly under royal control. For example, this was the case of Scandinavian towns such as Sigtuna, Sweden. Kings could profit a great deal from taxing trade goods that moved in and out of cities. When a town was under royal control, all fines from court cases went into the king's treasury. Often a king also received rents from numerous buildings in the cities under his rule. Furthermore, as kings increased their power over larger and larger areas, they found that cities were convenient centers from which to run the government. It was during the High Middle Ages that the idea of having a capital city took shape in Europe.

Royal control benefited townspeople, too. People who lived in a royal city were automatically free from serfdom: they were not required to work on a lord's land or pay the many fees that serfs owed their lords. In some parts of Europe, a serf could become free simply by moving to a city and living there for a year and a day.

A number of cities were under the rule of a count or other lord, who was usually a royal vassal. The French city of Troyes was ruled by the count of Champagne, a vassal of the king of France. The count received the same taxes, fines, and rents that royal cities paid to the king. Often both kings and counts encouraged trade and prosperity by guaranteeing protection for merchants traveling to the cities under their control.

Lionello d'Este, the duke of Ferrara, ran his city free of royal control.

GOVERNING A GREAT CITY: VENICE

The greatest medieval republic was the city of Venice. Its government evolved slowly over many centuries, taking its final form in the years from 1297 to 1310.

A duke, called the doge (DOHJ), was the head of state. His actual powers were quite limited, but he had great influence and prestige. His presence was required at every meeting of every branch of the government. Six dogal councillors assisted him and made certain that he did not try to increase his authority. These councillors were elected three at a time and stayed in office for only eight months. Together the doge, the dogal councillors, and the city's three chief judges fulfilled such duties as overseeing elections and making recommendations to the Senate.

The Senate was a body of 120 men elected for one-year terms, plus as many as 155 other officials. Some of these officials had the right to vote in the Senate, but some did not. The Senate dealt with foreign affairs, finances, trade policies, and other issues. It levied taxes and customs duties, declared war, and made the laws of the republic.

The senators and most other government officials were chosen by the Great Council. This council was made up of all Venetian noblemen aged twenty-five and above. Besides electing senators, judges, admirals, ambassadors, provincial governors, the doge, and others, the Great Council also debated political issues and approved the decisions of the Senate.

The members of the Great Council were under constant scrutiny by the Council of Ten. This group was formed in 1310 to protect the republic from enemies both outside and within. The ten councillors were elected for one-year terms by the Great Council. The Ten saw that swift and ruthless punishment was dealt to any noble who abused his position, conspired to overthrow Venice's government, or plotted with foreign powers. The Council of Ten's authority was held in check by the Great Council, which could if necessary refuse to elect anyone to the Council of Ten.

The common people of Venice had little say in their government's decisions. However, during the Middle Ages they would gather in the city's main square to voice their approval or disapproval of the government's actions. The election of the doge also had to be ratified by the assembled people. Before a new doge took office, he was presented to the people with the words, "Here is your doge, if he is pleasing to you." This presentation gradually became a mere formality, although it continued to be greeted with cheers.

Venice, situated on a group of islands near the Adriatic Sea, was one of medieval Europe's most powerful cities. The great trading center was called the Queen of Cities.

In northern and central Italy it was not unusual for cities to have nothing to do with royalty at all. Officially most of them were ruled by the Holy Roman Emperor. But in practice many were countries in their own right, sometimes themselves controlling other cities, along with rural areas.

These city-states were governed in various ways. For example, during the twelfth century many places hired a professional administrator, called a podestà, to run the city for a certain amount of time. Usually the podestà was from another region so that he could not be easily swayed by any of the different factions in the town he was overseeing. Other cities, such as Florence and Venice, were republics, where government officials were elected. During the thirteenth and fourteenth centuries some Italian city-states came to be ruled by independent dukes. These dukedoms usually became hereditary; for example, the dukes of Milan came from the Visconti family, and those of Ferrara from the Este family.

FREE CITIES

A striking feature of life in a large number of Italian cities was the commune, an institution that probably began in the eleventh century. A commune was a unified body that acted as the "voice" of the entire town. All the members of the commune were businessmen, who swore an oath of loyalty to one another and to the city. They pledged to defend their rights even against their lord. Members of the nobility and the clergy were usually not allowed to join the commune.

The Italian commune was imitated all over Europe. Numerous cities received charters of freedom from their lords, granting the right of self-government in return for an annual tax payment. In

The citizens of a city in Flanders (now Belgium) receive their charter of freedom.

England, where communes were known as boroughs, King John granted London the right to elect its own sheriff in 1199 and the right to elect its own mayor in 1215.

A number of bishops and other churchmen preached strongly against the communes, which they believed were destroying the social order. Many other lords seemed glad to see their subjects forming communes. A city that was a free commune attracted a great deal of business; the more business prospered, the more tax money the lord received.

Most free cities in northwest Europe were governed by a mayor and a town council. These officials served for set terms (the mayor of London's term of office was one year). At the end of this time they might choose their own successors. Alternatively, the new mayor and councilmen might be elected by a group of leading citizens, for instance the master craftsmen of the city. In all medieval European towns, the right to vote was limited to a relatively small number of people, usually the wealthiest men of the community. Even in a free city, there were many inequalities.

3

INSIDE THE CITY WALLS

The violence of the early Middle Ages taught town dwellers the importance of strong defenses. For this reason most towns were protected by tall, thick stone walls. Many cities kept growing after their walls were constructed. Often this meant that new buildings had to take the place of gardens and orchards inside the city walls. Sometimes a new wall had to be built to surround and protect the homes and businesses that had grown up outside the original wall. Only one major medieval city was not protected by walls: Venice, surrounded by water and possessing the strongest navy in Europe, needed no other defense.

A number of cities had not only walls but also a fortress or castle. In many cases the castle had been there first, and the city had grown up around it. The city of Edinburgh, for example, took shape along the road that led between the king of Scotland's castle and Holyrood Abbey. (An abbey was a large monastery or convent headed by an abbot or abbess.) Sometimes a city without a castle decided that it needed greater protection from enemies and built a new fortress for the purpose. In 1202 the king of France ordered the

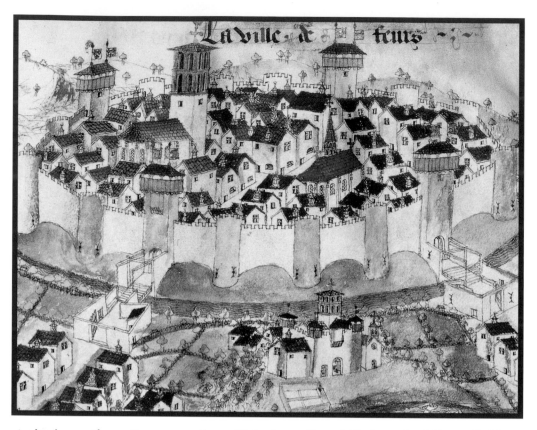

A city in southern France nestles within its walls, while farm buildings, fields, and a monastery sprawl across the surrounding countryside.

building of a castle in Paris at a place by the Seine River where he thought the city's defenses were especially weak. The king himself did not live in the castle (he had a palace elsewhere in the city), but he did store his treasure there.

STREETS AND SQUARES

Visitors to a medieval city—perhaps attending a fair—entered through gates in the city's wall. (They might have to cross a drawbridge over a moat first.) Inside the wall they found streets lined with homes and businesses. Some buildings were painted red and blue or decorated in other ways. Signs with colorful pictures hung over the doorways of shops and taverns. Goods of all kinds were laid out on display on counters in front of the shops. Businesses of the same sort usually clustered together in the same part of the city or even on the same street. Visitors, as well as city residents, avoided the neighborhoods of the butchers and tanners as much as possible—these trades produced extremely unpleasant smells.

Streets were crowded with pedestrians, horses, and carts. Cats, dogs, geese, chickens, pigs, sheep, and cattle were also likely to be in the street. Many cities had at least two main thoroughfares, often running east to west and north to south. These tended to be fairly wide and straight. Other streets, however, usually were not. Some Paris streets were so narrow that only one person at a time could walk down them. Most streets in medieval cities were unpaved, muddy, foul, and smelly. In 1185 the king of France could no longer stand the odor coming from the mud, and he gave orders for the main streets of Paris to be paved with stones.

Throughout the medieval city were open squares, often in front of churches and generally unpaved. Sometimes a group of houses was built around a small square. Usually a city had at least one square large enough to serve as a gathering place for much of the population. Ten thousand or more people at a time could assemble in the square in front of Venice's Church of Saint Mark.

On the square in front of Notre Dame Cathedral in Paris, a pork market was held once a week. Most cities had various open-air markets, sometimes held in a church square and sometimes held in a district of the city dedicated to fairs and markets. Paris had a famous market called Les Halles, where the king had constructed

This fifteenth-century manuscript page shows tradesmen at work along a French city street. From left to right, there are tailors, furriers, a barber, and a grocer.

EVERYDAY LIFE IN MEDIEVAL EUROPE

A busy market in fifteenth-century Italy. Most of the women merchants are keeping hold of their distaffs and spindles so that they can spin between sales.

two large buildings to shelter greengrocers, grain merchants, and dealers in small goods. Other towns also had permanent market buildings as well as open areas where visiting merchants could set up temporary stalls and tents.

GLORY TO GOD

Every neighborhood had its own parish church. Medieval churches were not only places of worship but also social centers. Meetings of various kinds, including town councils, were often held in churches. There was a church service every three hours, beginning at dawn. The ringing of the bells before each of these services marked the passage of time for city dwellers.

Many churches were dedicated to particular saints. The saints were people who had lived exceptionally holy lives and who had the power to perform miracles. Since God was often felt to be unreachable by ordinary humans, many Christians prayed to saints to "speak to" God in their behalf.

When seeking a saint's help, a person often prayed before a picture or statue of the saint or, if possible, at the saint's tomb or at a shrine to the saint. Some shrines housed relics—physical remains (usually bones)—of the saint. Holy relics had a great reputation for miraculous powers. During the Middle Ages people often traveled great distances on pilgrimages to visit churches that housed the relics of saints.

Some of the most splendid churches in medieval cities were the cathedrals. During the twelfth century a new style of architecture became very popular and was used for many cathedrals (as well as other churches). This style later came to be known as Gothic architecture. Recently developed engineering techniques allowed stone structures to soar to lofty heights. This was very effective in the new cathedrals, where tall, pointed arches and other features naturally drew worshipers' eyes up toward heaven.

The new style of building also allowed large windows to be set into the high walls of the cathedrals. Since colored glass was actually easier to produce at this time than perfectly clear glass, the church designers made a virtue of necessity and created stained glass windows. At first, pieces of glass were joined together in lead frames to make abstract designs. But very soon it was realized that pictures could be made with the colored glass. Stained glass windows illustrating episodes from the Bible and other religious scenes became an important feature of churches from then on. For many worshipers, who could neither read nor understand most of the

Gothic cathedrals, with their tall, pointed arches, splendid windows, and fine works of art, helped draw people's thoughts toward God.

church service (which was in Latin), these windows were their version of the Bible.

Probably the world's most famous Gothic cathedral is Notre Dame in Paris. Notre Dame, like many other Gothic cathedrals, took close to a century to complete. The work was done in stages, often halting for a time when money ran out. Yet no expense was spared in cathedral construction. Lords, prominent citizens, and groups of craftspeople all made donations to finance the new churches and their beautiful windows. These masterpieces in stone and glass not only glorified God but were also monuments to civic pride.

THE HALLS OF LEARNING

In addition to their other functions, cathedrals were centers of learning. Most had a cathedral school, originally organized by the bishop to educate future priests. In the eleventh century cathedral schools began to take additional students—sons of nobles, merchants, and other well-to-do citizens. By the twelfth century there were many renowned cathedral schools in Europe. Each school tended to have its own specialties, and students often traveled from school to school over the course of many years.

This was the beginning of the European university, a creation of the Middle Ages. By 1200 five great universities were taking form in the cities of Salerno and Bologna (Italy), Montpellier and Paris (France), and Oxford (England). By 1250 Europe boasted a total of twenty-two universities. Some were particularly noted for teaching law, others for medicine, and others for philosophy and religion.

University students might be as young as fourteen. For much of the Middle Ages they did not live in dormitories or study in libraries;

A lecture at the University of Paris, around the year 1400. By this time university classes had become more formal than in earlier centuries. The professor teaches from a raised platform, while students sitting on benches take notes.

universities at this time had few if any permanent buildings. Instead classes were held in the homes of professors, or even in rooms over taverns. Students sat on the floor, listening to lectures and debating points of logic, all in Latin. At night they returned to rented rooms to

BROTHERS OF THE BRIDGE

The eleventh century saw the beginning of a wave of bridge building in western Europe. Ferries were becoming inadequate to deal with the increasing number of medieval travelers, especially merchants with their carts and trains of packhorses. Local lords, who profited from tolls collected at river crossings on their lands, realized that bridges could be a source of needed cash. The Church recognized bridges as a great help to travelers, especially pilgrims, and supported their construction.

In the twelfth century a group of devout men in southern France dedicated themselves to the good work of bridge building. These "Brothers of the Bridge" were responsible for the famous bridge of Avignon, which had a combination chapel and toll booth at one end. Even though the bridge became unusable in the 1600s, French children still sing and dance to an old folksong about it, "Sur le pont d'Avignon" ("On the Bridge of Avignon").

Another medieval bridge later made famous in song was London Bridge. It was completed in 1209 and was the only bridge over the Thames River until 1750. Nineteen stone arches, each of them slightly different from the others, supported it. At one place in the bridge there was a gap covered by a drawbridge. If the city was ever attacked, this drawbridge could be raised to prevent enemies from crossing. Drawbridges had long been used over castle moats, but this is the first known use of the drawbridge at a river crossing.

As with bridges in other medieval towns, there were many houses and shops on London Bridge. A bridge was a good place to live and work, because water could easily be drawn from the river. Medieval city dwellers dumped their trash and sewage into the rivers, so waste disposal was also more convenient for people who lived on bridges. Unfortunately, this added to the unhealthiness of city living conditions in general.

London Bridge, with its many arches and houses, can be seen in the background of this view of the city in the late 1400s. In the foreground, King Henry VII sits in the White Tower, part of the Tower of London today.

read or copy manuscripts by candlelight. After six years or so of study, they might take an examination and receive a license to teach. They might also become churchmen, lawyers, or doctors, or enter the service of a king or noble. No matter what career path a university student ended up choosing, one thing was certain: the pursuit of higher education was becoming a major element of city life, and of European culture in general.

4
HOME SWEET HOME

Most houses in medieval cities were built of wood, though some were of brick or stone. They could be up to four stories tall and were often narrow. As wooden houses aged, they tended to sag and lean. Sometimes they leaned so badly that the tops of houses on opposite sides of a street almost touched!

In poorer neighborhoods, several families lived in each house, renting their rooms from the house's owner. A very poor family might have only one room. This was often where they worked as well as where they cooked, ate, slept, and so on. If the father or mother was a weaver by trade, the loom probably took up most of the family's quarters.

In general, for city people their home was also their place of business. An independent craftsperson would have a shop and workshop on the ground floor of a house, and the family would live on the upper floors.

Wealthy merchants could have very large and splendid homes. In Venice, for example, such a house was usually three stories tall. The first level was given over to business. The front entrance, facing the water, had a quay or dock. (Venice had canals instead of streets, boats and ships instead of carts and trains of packhorses.) The central doorway led into a spacious hall where goods could be unloaded,

This painting by Simon Bening shows the inside of a wealthy merchant's home in Flanders around 1500.

counted, and inspected. On either side of this, and half its height, were storerooms. The merchant had his offices on an in-between level above the storerooms. On the second floor was a large central hall that was often used as a showroom for merchandise. It was also the place where banquets, weddings, and other gatherings were held. To the sides of this hall were the family's living quarters. The top floor provided rooms for servants and employees.

ALL THE COMFORTS OF HOME?

Even for wealthy families, living conditions were not what we would think of as comfortable. Fireplaces were the only source of heat and often the main source of light. Oiled parchment was the most common window covering, and windows were usually small and narrow to begin with. Oil lamps and smoky tallow candles tended to be lit only after dark.

The main room of a private house, sometimes called the solar, was where the family dined. It contained benches, one or two cupboards for storing dishes and utensils, and a trestle table (which was only set up at mealtimes). In well-to-do homes, panels of dyed or embroidered cloth hung on the walls. Beginning in the early 1300s, tapestries—more elaborate wall hangings—became available to the wealthy. At this time, too, rugs began to be common in European cities; before this floors were usually covered only with rushes, sometimes with fragrant herbs and flowers added.

The kitchen was often behind the solar. The kitchen's main feature was a huge fireplace, where all the cooking was done. There was a long worktable, a large vat for water, and a spice cabinet. Of

SPICE IT UP!

In the Middle Ages spices were a luxury. Merchants who traded in spices could make huge profits. These merchants and other well-to-do city dwellers enjoyed highly spiced food. From near Venice comes a recipe for a spice mixture that could be used "for all foods": one part black pepper, one part cinnamon, one part ginger, one-quarter part saffron, and one-eighth part cloves.

Another spicy medieval recipe, this time from England, is for a kind of ginger candy: Boil a quart of honey, and skim off any scum that rises to the top. Remove from heat and add a pinch of saffron, a pinch of white pepper, and a few pinches each of ginger and cinnamon. Thoroughly stir in plain, white bread-crumbs—enough to make the honey a very thick mass. Let the mixture cool slightly, then pour it out onto a flat surface and pat it into a square or rectangle. When it is cooled completely, cut it into small squares, stick a whole clove into each square, and enjoy!

course the kitchen also contained pots, cauldrons, trivets, mortars and pestles, spoons, and a number of other cooking utensils. Many houses had small gardens to supply the kitchen with herbs and vegetables.

The great writer Christine de Pisan (1363–1430), daughter of a doctor from Venice, presents a copy of one of her books to the queen of France. The queen's richly canopied bed is similar to the beds in which wealthy townspeople slept.

Bedroom furniture included a washstand, a chest, and perhaps a table and a few chairs. Adults slept in huge canopied beds; children's beds were smaller and plainer. There were no closets for clothes. Garments were stored in chests or hung up on hooks on the wall or on a rod behind the bed. People slept naked or in their underclothes.

Cleanliness was a challenge in the medieval city. Water for drinking, cooking, and washing had to be carried from a well outside the house; often many houses shared a single well. People generally bathed once a week at most. Fleas, bedbugs, and lice were constant problems. To go to the bathroom, most people had to use an outhouse in the yard. At night, they could use a chamber pot that was kept under the bed. Some homes might have a garderobe, a kind of indoor outhouse, off the bedroom. Garderobes often emptied into nearby canals, streams, or ditches, contributing to the city's smelly and unhealthy atmosphere.

It was hard to keep clean in the Middle Ages. Hair lice were a common problem. Here a man gets a thorough scrubbing.

5

CITY FOLKS

With the growth of cities in the Middle Ages, a new class of people became increasingly important in European society. These people were not rulers or nobles with large landholdings, and they were not peasant farmers or common laborers. They were a middle class: merchants, bankers, doctors, lawyers, and skilled craftspeople. Middle-class property owners and master craftsmen—called bourgeois, burghers, burgesses, or similar names in much of northwest Europe—were a town's leading citizens. They paid a share of the borough's annual tax to the king and enjoyed a number of privileges in return, including the rights to vote and hold city offices.

Although burghers were highly influential, their numbers were relatively small. Most city residents were common working people with no say in how the city was run. Many of these people lived comfortably enough, but others were very poor. Some were unable to make a regular living and resorted to begging. This became a greater problem as increasing numbers of peasants left the countryside in the hope of gaining freedom and finding more profitable work in the towns.

Merchants such as these jewelers were part of the middle class that became so important in medieval cities. In addition to jewelry and objects plated with silver or gold, this shop sells precious stones. In the Middle Ages gemstones were not only valued for their beauty, but were also believed to have the power of curing or preventing various illnesses.

Hospitals began to appear in a number of medieval cities. These hospitals were usually established by the Church and run by monks and sometimes nuns. They not only treated sick people but also fed and clothed the poor. Some hospitals also provided food and shelter for pilgrims, and others cared for orphans. Saint Catherinc's Hospital in Paris gave free lodging to poor widows and young girls who came to the city looking for work. By 1180 Paris also had three colleges, which provided cheap housing for impoverished university students.

Doctors and patients in an Italian hospital

URBAN MELTING POTS

Medieval cities were meeting places for people of many nationalities. A city where the king held court would be visited from time to time by foreign ambassadors. If a city had a university, it attracted students from all over Europe. Pilgrims, too, journeyed to cities in a number of different countries. Other visitors or temporary residents in towns were traveling preachers and wandering entertainers.

Stone masons and carpenters build a medieval church.

Cities that were erecting new churches and cathedrals "imported" many of the skilled craftspeople needed for the construction. These workers, from a variety of places, often lived in temporary housing right in the cathedral yard. Master masons, master carpenters, bell founders, and window makers in particular traveled from building site to building site as their services were needed.

MARCO POLO

The most famous of all medieval merchants was Marco Polo. In 1271, at the age of seventeen, Marco Polo left Venice with his father and uncle. They were heading for China, which the two older men had already visited once. After a four-year journey the Polos reached China's eastern coast and the court of the emperor, Kublai Khan.

The emperor was extremely impressed with Marco Polo's abilities and took the young Venetian into his service. Over the course of the next seventeen years Marco was given numerous diplomatic missions, which took him not only all over China but also to India, Persia, Tibet, Burma (today's Myanmar), and Vietnam. Everywhere he went, he carefully observed and remembered scenery, people's customs, and details of local trade.

At last the Polos grew homesick, and in 1292 they set out for Venice. Arriving home after an arduous journey over land and sea, they were greeted with astonishment and disbelief. The tales they told of their travels and their long stay in the East were incredible. But the rich robes and fabulous jewels they brought back, proof of the wealth of the East, made a deep impression on their fellow Venetians.

As for Marco, he eventually turned the story of his adventures into a book. *The Travels of Marco Polo* became a medieval best-seller. Aside from describing the wonders of the East, Marco's book provided extremely accurate geographical information. For centuries his book was referred to by mapmakers and explorers, including Christopher Columbus.

Marco Polo died in 1324. It is said that his last words were, "I did not write half of what I saw."

Trade was the force that brought the most visitors of all into the medieval city. The great fairs held twice a year in the French city of Troyes attracted merchants not only from all of France but also from Spain, Italy, Germany, Flanders, England, Scotland, and Scandinavia. Venice had so many foreign merchants visiting on a regular basis that in the early 1300s the city began to construct permanent business centers for them. Venetian merchants themselves voyaged to most of the known world, everywhere from England to North Africa to Constantinople and beyond. Many Venetians and others lived and did business in foreign cities for years at a time.

Medieval cities commonly had large Jewish populations. Church law prohibited Jews from owning land and from earning their living by manufacturing or selling goods to the general public. At the same time Christians were generally forbidden to make loans and charge interest. Jews were therefore able to play an important role as bankers and moneylenders in many cities.

City governments were often tolerant of Jews, especially when this proved profitable. But all too often during the Middle Ages, a ruler needing money would expel the Jews from the area under his rule, confiscating all of their property and belongings. This happened in Paris in 1182. Sixteen years later the banished Jews were allowed to return to the city, but only after paying a tax to the king.

Even worse, Jews were sometimes targets of extreme violence. For example, in 1190, 150 Jewish men, women, and children were killed in the city of York, England. Even in the international atmosphere of the medieval city, the Christian majority had difficulty understanding and accepting religious differences.

6
TAKING CARE OF
BUSINESS

edieval cities were not only centers of commerce, they were also centers of manufacturing. Some cities specialized in particular products. Many towns of Flanders were noted for their woolen cloth; the Italian city of Lucca specialized in silk cloth. Milan, Italy, was a source of armor, crossbows, and other military equipment. Venice was famous for its glass, used for windows, mirrors, goblets, beads, and more.

The citizens of a prosperous medieval town might work at more than a hundred different crafts and trades. In a large city like Paris the number of different occupations could be close to two hundred. Many trades were family affairs, with husband, wife, and children all sharing in the work. Sometimes husband and wife worked at two different trades, however. Widows and single women often supported themselves (and sometimes their children, too) through crafts or various businesses.

In much of Europe during the High Middle Ages, women worked at almost as many kinds of jobs as men did. Only a few professions were totally closed to women at this time: they could not be sailors, notaries, lawyers, or priests. But we have records from around

1300 that tell of women—especially in France, Germany, and England—who were merchants, money changers, jewelers, goldsmiths, artists, stone masons, entertainers, tavern keepers, shoemakers,

Glassblowers at work in the fifteenth century

A blacksmith at her forge

leather workers, shield makers, archers, gatekeepers, millers, blacksmiths, brewers, wine dealers, food sellers, fishmongers, bakers, ped-
dlers, dyers, yarn makers, wool weavers, linen workers, tailors,
dressmakers, hat makers, furriers, hairdressers, candle makers, spice
dealers, pharmacists, doctors, surgeons, and barbers (who not only
cut hair but also performed minor surgery and set broken bones). As
household servants, laundresses, nurses, wax dealers, silk spinners,
silk weavers, embroiderers, and lace makers, Parisian women out-
numbered men in 1292. Unfortunately, as in so many other times

THE COMPLAINT OF THE WOMEN SILK WEAVERS

Chrétien de Troyes (1135–1190) was one of the most popular writers in medieval France. He wrote several long poems that told stories about King Arthur and the knights and ladies of his court. Chrétien was a city dweller, though, and even in his courtly tales he included vivid descriptions of urban life. The following selection, translated from his *Yvain, or The Knight of the Lion*, vividly portrays the difficult working and living conditions of many townspeople:

> *Always we weave the silken cloth;*
> *Never are we ourselves well clothed.*
> *Always we are poor and in distress,*
> *And always we suffer hunger and thirst,*
> *Never knowing what it is to succeed*
> *Or even to have enough to eat:*
> *In the morning we share a little bread,*
> *And in the evening even less.*
> *. . .*
> *We are so poor, we barely live,*
> *While that man for whom we slave*
> *Enriches himself from our plight.*
> *We stay awake a great part of the night*
> *And all the day making money for him,*
> *For he threatens to break our limbs*
> *If we rest even with good cause,*
> *And so we dare not stop or pause.*

and places, medieval women routinely earned less money than men, even for the same work.

Women who didn't work for pay still worked hard, raising children and keeping house. Even with a servant or two to help, household chores were time-consuming and often demanded a great deal of strength from the medieval housewife. Only women in very wealthy families avoided physical labor completely.

GUILDS

During the Middle Ages people who worked at the same craft or trade typically belonged to a guild. Guilds set standards for products and workmanship, regulated wages and employment practices, paid for members' funerals, and looked after members' interests in other ways.

Around 1300, Paris had five guilds whose members were all women; Cologne (Germany) had four. (In both cities, these women-only guilds were primarily dedicated to various stages in the making of silk cloth.) There were many guilds in a number of cities where women were very active in their own right, even though most members were male. In other guilds, women could not be admitted unless they were wives, widows, or, sometimes, daughters of male guild members. It seems that virtually the only guilds that were completely closed to women throughout Europe were the guilds of the great merchants.

One of the guild's most important functions was to regulate the training of apprentices, or student craftspeople. Depending on the difficulty of the craft, an apprentice spent from four to twelve years learning his or her trade from a master. During this time the

An apprentice alchemist stirs his brew while his master reads the "recipe." Alchemists were medieval chemists who believed they could find a recipe for turning base metals into gold.

apprentice usually lived in the master's home, and the master supplied the apprentice with food and clothing as well as training. The apprentice not only learned from but also assisted the master, even helping out with household chores when necessary.

When apprentices finished their training, they had to prove to the guild that they knew their craft or trade, and they had to show that they had the money or tools to go into business for themselves. They swore that they were loyal and careful and that they would practice their profession honestly and responsibly. Finally, after paying a fee, they were accepted as masters and full members of their guild.

HARD WORK

Not all workers in medieval cities belonged to guilds. Some trades did not have guilds. Some people worked at their craft, even training apprentices, without ever belonging to the guild for it. But most city dwellers did not have specialized, skilled crafts or trades. Unskilled laborers probably made up the majority of workers in the medieval city. Often they had no regular employment, but took whatever jobs were available, day by day. In addition, many townspeople were involved in agriculture. Every morning they left the city to work in fields, orchards, vineyards, or pastures outside the city walls. They returned to their urban homes before watchmen or guards closed the city gates for the night.

However they earned their living, most people in medieval cities worked very hard. The average workday was from ten to fourteen hours long. Unless there was a holiday during the week, Sunday was the only day off—and, as many preachers complained, large numbers of people preferred to rest and relax on Sunday rather than attend church.

7

GROWING UP IN A MEDIEVAL CITY

I n the Middle Ages all babies were born at home. During labor, a city woman was often assisted by a midwife. She was also visited and encouraged by various female relatives, friends, and neighbors. (No men were allowed to be present.) In a well-to-do household, dishes of candied fruits and nuts were put out for the benefit of these visitors, and some of the family's best possessions were displayed in the woman's room.

Even in wealthy families, childbirth was difficult and dangerous. No one at this time knew about the risk of infection or about ways to prevent it. If something went wrong while a woman was giving birth, there was little the midwife could do. Sometimes she would whisper magical chants into the mother's ears, even though the Church disapproved of such things. Many babies and mothers died during or soon after birth.

If everything went well, the midwife immediately washed the newborn baby and then wrapped it securely in swaddling bands. (These bands were tight enough to keep the baby from moving, for fear that too much movement would cause its arms and legs to

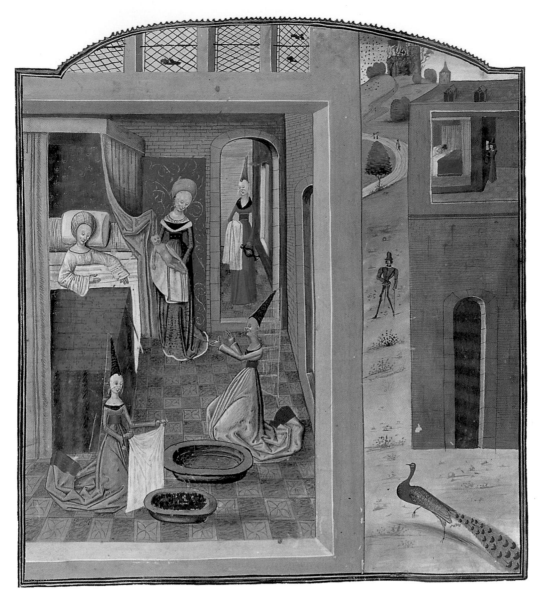

This painting from a fifteenth-century manuscript shows a midwife drying off a newborn baby before placing him in his mother's arms.

twist out of shape.) Then the baby was shown to its father for the first time.

Soon afterward, in a Christian family, the baby was taken to church to be baptized. A female relative carried the child, followed by the father, the godparents, the midwife, and various friends and family members; the mother, however, remained at home. During the ceremony a priest anointed the baby with oil and dipped him or her into holy water. The godparents assisted, giving their promise to see that the child was raised according to the teachings of the Church. Townspeople often liked to choose rich and important citizens to be their children's godparents.

Back at home, the newborn was placed in a wooden cradle at its mother's bedside. Nearly all medieval babies were breast-fed, but well-to-do city dwellers generally hired a servant, called a nurse, for this purpose. The nurse fed and bathed the baby every three hours.

A mother rocks her baby in its cradle. The five-pointed star carved at the foot of the cradle was a powerful symbol of protection during the Middle Ages.

CHILDHOOD

When babies were old enough to sit up, they were released from their swaddling. From then on they wore adult-style clothes. About half of all children died before they reached the age of five. Those who lived spent their early years mostly in play. Children in well-off families might have tops, wooden swords, hobby horses, stilts, marbles, dolls made out of wood or clay, and similar toys. Other children had to use their imaginations and whatever they could find—sticks, leaves, flowers, horseshoes, blocks of wood, and even bread crusts. Many children had fun with balloons made from the bladders of recently slaughtered pigs. Like adults, children might enjoy games such as chess, checkers, backgammon, dice games, lawn bowling, wrestling, and blindman's buff.

A group of boys enjoy a game known as frog-in-the-middle.

HUNT THE SLIPPER
A MEDIEVAL GAME

This game was enjoyed by both children and adults in medieval towns and cities, where cobbling (repairing shoes) was a common trade.

To play hunt the slipper, the players need to sit in a tight circle on the floor or in chairs. One player, called Slipper Soul, sits or stands in the middle of the circle. She or he should be holding a slipper or shoe. While the other players pretend to be cobblers hard at work, Slipper Soul says:

Cobbler, cobbler,
Mend my shoe!
Make it all anew.
Three stitches will do!

With that, Slipper Soul hands the shoe or slipper to one of the players in the circle, then closes his or her eyes for several seconds. The other players pass the shoe from one to another behind their backs. When Slipper Soul's eyes are open again, everyone continues to pretend that they are passing the shoe around the circle. Slipper Soul must guess who actually has it. When that person is identified, he or she takes the shoe into the middle of the circle, becoming the next Slipper Soul, and the game begins all over again!

Boys attending grammar school in the mid-fourteenth century.

Around the age of seven children began to prepare for their adult roles. Some boys and girls in medieval cities attended primary school, where they learned basic arithmetic and reading. Boys could go on to more advanced studies at a cathedral school, and then perhaps at a university. For girls, the rest of their education usually took place at home and focused on cooking, cloth making, and other skills needed to run a household and care for a family. However, a number of girls as well as boys began an apprenticeship sometime between the ages of seven and twelve. Many others went straight to work, doing whatever was necessary to assist their parents.

Childhood was short, but so was life. Most girls married when they were teenagers and were soon raising children of their own. After only ten or fifteen years of marriage, they might well find themselves widows, for husbands were typically ten, twenty, or thirty years older than their wives. During the Middle Ages fifty was considered a ripe old age.

8
FEAST DAYS AND PLAYS

City life was not all work and no play. There were many holidays throughout the year when everyday work ceased. Most of these holidays were Christian feast days, although sometimes the celebrations did not seem very religious. Venice celebrated the Feast of the Purification of the Virgin Mary (February 2) with boat races on the city's Grand Canal. On the Feast of the Holy Innocents (December 28) French choirboys switched places with cathedral officials and conducted the church services. Another holiday saw low-ranking priests wearing their robes inside out, nibbling sausages in church, and braying like donkeys during the worship service!

As with Christians today the most important holidays were Christmas and Easter. Before each there was a period of many weeks when people were supposed to turn their thoughts away from worldly pleasures, spend extra time in prayer, and purify themselves of sin as much as possible. When Christmas and Easter finally arrived, everyone celebrated as lavishly as they could afford to. Wealthy families had elaborate feasts, serving up to ten courses.

As minstrels play and servants offer platters of food, a group of fourteenth-century nobles and churchmen enjoy an elaborate feast.

Such feasts often included entertainment by musicians, singers, jugglers, and acrobats.

Plays were another favorite holiday entertainment in medieval cities. In the church services for Christmas and Easter, priests often acted out parts of the Bible stories of Jesus' birth and resurrection. These mini-plays were all in Latin, but they were so popular with worshipers that longer plays were eventually presented in French, German, and English. By the thirteenth century Christmas and Easter plays were being given outdoors in front of the church. The plays portrayed episodes from the Bible, such as the story of Adam and Eve, as well as stories of the lives and miracles of various saints.

THE BOAR'S HEAD CAROL
A SONG FROM MEDIEVAL ENGLAND

The words of this carol were first written down in the 1400s at the University of Oxford. Students and professors probably sang it as a procession brought in the main dish of the Christmas feast, a boar's head bedecked with garlands of greenery. Versions of "The Boar's Head Carol" are sometimes still sung at Christmastime today.

Before me I bear the head, *
Singing praises to the Lord.

The boar's head in hands I bring,
With garlands gay and birds singing.
I pray you all to help me sing,
You here at this gathering.

Before me I bear the head,
Singing praises to the Lord.

The boar's head, I understand,
Is the chief dish served in all this land.
And everywhere it may be found,
It is served with good mustard.

Before me I bear the head,
Singing praises to the Lord.

The boar's head, I dare well say,
Soon after Yuletide's twelfth day,
He takes his leave and goes away—
Then he has left our country.

Before me I bear the head,
Singing praises to the Lord.

*Words in italics were originally in Latin.

In the English city of York, players enact the biblical story of the Sacrifice of Abraham. Nobles watch the procession from a platform elevated above the crowded square.

Comedy was combined with serious religious lessons so that the watchers would stay interested.

A number of English towns gradually developed cycles of plays that dramatized all the major events in the Bible, from the Creation to the Last Judgment. These play cycles came to be presented in squares and marketplaces around the feast of Corpus Christi (fifty-four days after Easter), which was celebrated with splendid processions through the city streets. Each individual play was produced by a specific guild, with guild members acting all the parts. In these English towns and in other medieval European cities, theater was evolving into the art form we know today.

CHAUCER'S URBAN PILGRIMS

Geoffrey Chaucer, a resident of London, was one of the greatest writers in English literature. He was born around 1340 and died in 1400. His most famous book is *The Canterbury Tales*, in which a group of people on a pilgrimage to the Shrine of Saint Thomas à Becket in Canterbury entertain one another by telling stories. Several of the pilgrims are typical city dwellers; among them are the Merchant, the Clerk, the Five Guildsmen, and the Wife of Bath. Here, adapted into modern English, are Chaucer's descriptions of these urban travelers:

THE MERCHANT

A merchant was there with a forked beard;
Richly clothed, high on his horse he sat.
On his head was an imported beaver-fur hat.
His boots were buckled most carefully.
He spoke his views very solemnly,
Always looking to the increase of his earnings.
He wished the sea kept safe more than anything.
. . .
This worthy man could use his head,
And no one knew if he was in debt,
So discreetly did he do his business,
With bargains and with making loans.

THE CLERK

A clerk from Oxford was there also,
Who began to study logic long ago.

A portrait of Geoffrey Chaucer

His horse was just as thin as a rake;
And he was not right fat, I undertake,
But looked hollow and full of care.
His outer cloak was all threadbare.

. . .

He would rather have by the head of his bed
Twenty books, bound in black or red,
Of Aristotle and his philosophy,
Than rich robes or music to make merry.
For all that he was a philosopher,
He had very little gold in his coffer;
But all he received that his friends lent,
On books and on learning it was spent,
And he would pray for the souls' ease
Of those who gave to him for his studies.
In thinking he took most care and most heed.
He spoke not one word more than he'd need,
And that was said in proper form and reverence,
And short and sweet, full of deep significance.
Full of moral virtue was his speech;
And gladly would he learn, and gladly teach.

THE FIVE GUILDSMEN

A haberdasher and a carpenter,
A weaver, a dyer, and a rug maker—
They all wore the badge and garb bestowed
On members of a tradesmen's brotherhood.

. . .

Each of them seemed a fair burgess
To sit in a guildhall on the dais.
Every one, on account of his wisdom,
Was well suited to be a councilman.
As for property and income, they had plenty—
And with this their wives would well agree,

Or else they were certain to complain;
It is very pleasant to be called "Madame,"
To walk at the head of holy-day processions,
And to wear a cloak as fine as a queen's!

THE WIFE OF BATH

From a suburb of Bath a good wife came,
But she was somewhat deaf, and that was a shame.
For making cloth she had such a bent,
She surpassed the famous weavers of Ghent.

. . .

Her many kerchiefs were finely textured—
I daresay that when she went to church,
They weighed ten pounds upon her head!
Her hose were of fine scarlet red,
Tightly tied, and her shoes were soft and new.
Bold was her face, and fair, and red of hue.
She was a worthy woman all her life.
As for husbands, she'd had five.

. . .

Three times she'd been to Jerusalem.
She had passed many a strange stream—
She had been to Rome and to Bologne,
To Saint James's shrine and to Cologne.

. . .

On an ambling horse she easily sat,
Bundled up well, on her head a hat
As wide around as a knight's shield,
A warm outer skirt from her hips to her heels.
On her feet she wore a pair of sharp spurs.
She laughed and joked with all the travelers.

The Wife of Bath

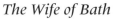

9

DISASTERS AND DISEASE

oday many people think of cities as dangerous places to live because of crime. There was crime in medieval cities, too, but there were also many more dangers from natural disasters, fire, warfare, and disease.

Most medieval towns were built next to rivers or the sea, and so flooding was a constant threat. In 1197 a terrible flood struck Paris, swamping the bridges and wiping out whole neighborhoods. The city suffered almost equally bad floods in 1206, 1220, and 1221. Towns in the Netherlands were flooded repeatedly; one thirteenth-century flood killed more than fifty thousand people living near the Dutch coast.

Fire was a huge danger in all medieval cities, for most urban buildings were built of wood and were crowded together. It took only one tipped-over candle or one spark from a fireplace to start a blaze that could destroy an entire neighborhood. When fire broke out, there were no professional firefighters to call on. Hastily organized bucket brigades were usually not enough to combat spreading flames.

Another constant threat was warfare. Italian city-states were frequently at war with one another. Other cities suffered in the

conflicts between nations, such as the Hundred Years' War between England and France. City walls were usually strong enough to resist attackers—unless the attackers were able to tunnel under the wall. However, if an enemy laid siege to the city, the residents did not have enough food to hold out indefinitely. Even in times of peace, it could be difficult to ensure a constant food supply for medieval towns. And where there was war and hunger, diseases always followed.

THE BLACK DEATH

The worst disease of the Middle Ages was the Black Death. This fearful plague swept through western Europe repeatedly during the fourteenth through the seventeenth centuries. The first wave of the disease, from 1347 to 1350, was the most devastating. Nearly every European city lost from one-quarter to two-thirds of its population. One chronicler recorded that from May to September 1348, 96,000 people died in Florence alone. Whole families were wiped out. There was no cure, and almost everyone who came down with the plague died from it, usually within four days.

Many city dwellers fled to the countryside, hoping to escape the dreaded disease. There was no escape; the Black Death struck rural villages and country mansions, too. By the time the epidemic ended, western Europe had lost roughly half its population.

Christian Europeans tried to understand why God had allowed such a terrible disease to suddenly kill so many. Sometimes

People in the Middle Ages were never free from the threat of war. In this manuscript painting, made in the twelfth century, Danes attack an English town.

they blamed foreigners or other "strangers" for bringing the plague to their city or country. The result was increased suspicion—and often persecution—of outsiders such as Jews and lepers (people who were already outcasts because they suffered from leprosy, a very serious skin disease).

The plague had other far-ranging effects on European society. Business and trade had come to a complete halt during the epidemic. When it was over, the economy had to be totally rebuilt. Labor was scarce and prices were high. Peasants and laborers demanded more rights and higher wages. Because of the scarcity and cost of labor, the Church permitted Christians to own non-Christian slaves. Governments passed laws that preserved the privileges of the upper class. Guilds tightened their rules, seeking to protect their members from competition, especially competition from women and others who would work for low wages.

After 1350 guilds and governments placed increasing limits on the work that women could do. For example, women were banned from being doctors, on the grounds that they could not receive a university medical license. (They were not allowed to attend universities at all.) Some women continued to work as doctors—often with great success—but they were frequently arrested, tried, and fined for practicing medicine without a license. Women were banned from many crafts, too, and admitted to fewer and fewer guilds. Not until the twentieth century would large numbers of women again enjoy the opportunity to work at the great variety of trades they had enjoyed in the cities of the High Middle Ages.

Europe's towns did make some strides forward following the Black Death of 1347–1350. Public health became a new area of government concern as cities explored various measures to keep diseases from spreading. City governments, at least in northern

Italy, had long been concerned with controlling pollution. Their efforts in this area increased, and there were efforts to improve sanitation as well.

Some towns never fully recovered from the disasters of the fourteenth century. Many others, however, went on to grow and thrive, continuing as centers of education, culture, and commerce. We can look to these medieval towns as the forerunners of the cities of today.

THE COUNTRYSIDE

1
PROTECTION AND OBEDIENCE

In the Middle Ages, very few people believed in any sort of equality. In every relationship, one party was superior to the other. Almost everyone in medieval Europe had a lord—someone more powerful and of higher social rank, to whom various services were owed.

A noble's lord was either a more powerful noble or a king. The lord granted land and gave protection to the lower-ranking noble, called a vassal. In return, the vassal pledged loyalty and obedience to the lord, particularly promising to fight in the lord's service. This military and political arrangement, which developed in the early Middle Ages, is known as feudalism.

Older history books often described feudalism as the social system of medieval Europe. It was thought that there was a feudal "chain of command" that stretched from the mightiest king all the way down to the lowliest peasant. More recently, though, historians have shown that feudal relationships affected only the top levels of medieval society, the kings and nobles.

The peasants, who made up the majority of medieval Europeans, were not part of this feudal network, which depended on military service and personal vows of loyalty. The relationship

between peasants and their lords, often called manorialism, was different. Manorialism was the basic economic system in much of Europe until the late Middle Ages. As in feudalism, peasants expected protection from their lord and were granted land by him. But instead of military service, peasants gave the lord their labor and the products of their labor.

Naturally, there were many variations in this pattern. Manorialism barely took hold in some parts of Europe, such as Frisia (today's Netherlands), Scandinavia, and Scotland. Even in places where the system was widespread, there could be major differences in the relationships between lords and peasants. And as the Middle Ages progressed, it became common for peasants to make cash payments to their lord instead of working for him.

In exchange for land and protection, peasants worked for the lord. Here, a peasant uses a scythe to mow the grass, an important summer chore. The grass will dry in the sun, making hay to feed the farm animals during wintertime.

2
THE LORD OF THE MANOR

A manor was an estate held by a lord. It was made up of the lord's demesne (deh-MAIN), which was his own land, and land held by peasant villagers. In return for their land, the villagers owed the lord various services or payments. A single manor might be made up of part of a village, an entire village, or more than one village.

The lord of the manor was usually a nobleman, but not always. Sometimes the lord was a high-ranking church official, such as a bishop. Some manors were held by noble widows and heiresses. Other estates belonged to abbeys, religious communities for men or women. In such a case, the lord of the manor was the abbot or abbess who headed the community.

Some lords, very minor knights or nobles, held only one manor. Some—like the Count of Champagne in what is now France—might have dozens and be powerful enough to rival kings. Most lords held several manors, which were often widely scattered through the countryside. The lord might visit each manor in turn, or he might live at the court of his overlord or in one of Europe's growing cities. Usually the lord did not live year-round on any one manor, unless that was all he held.

Lords did not work the land themselves, so they depended on their estates to provide them with grain, meat, cheese, and most of the rest of the food for their households. The manors gave them beeswax for their candles and sheep's wool and sometimes linen for their clothes. Rents, fees, fines, and sales of extra produce from

Life on the manor: making wine. While some peasants train and prune the vines, others harvest the grapes. One man stomps the grapes in a large wooden vat. In the foreground, the lord's agents are present to oversee the work.

the manors provided lords with money for their other wants and needs.

Some lords preferred to lease out their estates; this practice was especially common during the 1100s. For a fixed fee, a lord would rent either the demesne or the entire manor to someone else. The renter then managed the property and was entitled to all the taxes and services that were owed to the lord. Usually the renter was another lord, a businessman from an area town, a knight, or a rich peasant. Sometimes a group of peasants who lived on the manor joined together to lease it.

THE LORD'S AGENTS

Villagers rarely so much as caught a glimpse of their lord. Typically, the lord did not run the manor himself. Instead, there were three main officials who did this for him. In England these officials were known as the steward, the bailiff, and the reeve.

The steward (sometimes called a seneschal) was a knight or cleric who supervised all of the lord's manors, visiting each of them two or three times a year. The lord himself appointed the steward. One of the steward's most important duties when he was at a manor was to preside over the manorial court. Generally, all but the most serious crimes were tried in this court, which also settled disagreements between villagers and between villagers and the lord. Punishments from the manorial court were usually fines, which were paid to the lord.

The bailiff was the lord's representative on the manor. He was usually chosen by the steward. He might be a younger son from a noble family, or he might come from a well-to-do peasant family. In

A steward receives pledges of loyalty from the lord's free tenants.

either case, he was expected to be able to read and write. His major responsibility was to manage the demesne, making sure that the lord's crops and livestock were properly taken care of. He also made sure that the manor had all the supplies it needed to function—

everything from building materials to baskets. Anything that could not be produced on the manor itself had to be purchased in nearby towns. In addition, on many manors the bailiff was responsible for some aspects of law enforcement.

The reeve was a prosperous peasant who supervised the work for the lord. Usually the villagers elected him themselves, and he served a one-year term (he could be reelected repeatedly, though). It was also his duty to keep the demesne's accounts. Throughout the year he kept track of the villagers' workdays, the number of livestock, the size of the harvests, rents collected, and payments made. Since the reeve generally had no schooling and could neither read nor write, he recorded all these facts and figures by making marks on wooden tally sticks. At the end of the agricultural year (September 29 in England) he had to give a "reckoning" of the accounts to the steward or another official. The reeve was not paid for performing his office, but he was not required to do any other work for the lord.

Most manors also had a beadle, or hayward. This peasant assisted the reeve and was especially responsible for looking after the saving, storing, and sowing of the seeds for the demesne's grain crop. Other officers varied from estate to estate. But it seems that no manor, at least in England, was without ale tasters. These officials, who were often women, oversaw the quality and price of ale sold in the village. If they found that the ale was weak, its brewer had to pay the lord a fine.

3

A TYPICAL VILLAGE

At the center of a typical medieval village were peasant houses and community buildings. Surrounding them were the fields where crops such as grain, peas, and beans were grown. Beyond the fields stretched meadows and woodlands. Throughout much of western Europe, the village farmland was divided into three large fields. Peasant landholders had long strips of land in each. (Long strips were easiest to plow.) Every year one field was left fallow, one was planted in the fall, and one was

Wharram Percy, a medieval village in England

planted in the spring. Cattle, sheep, and horses were allowed to graze in the fields after the crops were harvested.

HUMBLE HOMES

Peasant dwellings ranged from tiny one-room cottages to high-ceilinged longhouses divided into four or five sections. They were not very solidly constructed—records tell of burglars easily smashing through the flimsy walls. Village houses often had to be rebuilt every thirty to forty years.

In England each house had a yard, or toft, enclosed by a ditch or fence. A family might have storage sheds and other outbuildings in the toft. If the family had chickens, pigs, a cow, or ox, the animals would have pens in the toft and would also graze there. Stretching back from the toft was the croft, a garden of about half an acre. This was where the family raised its vegetables. Some households also grew apple, pear, or cherry trees in the croft.

Often one end of the house had a byre, or barn, attached so that the family's livestock would be safe and sheltered during the winter. (The animals' body heat also helped keep the human residents of the house warm.) The other end might be partitioned off to form a storeroom.

The house's dirt floors were strewn with rushes, straw, or, on special occasions, herbs and wildflowers. Usually there were only

This plan of a typical English manor shows the village's three large fields, the lord's demesne, the manor house with the church nearby, and the homes of the villagers. Here, the crofts are small fields separate from the peasants' houses. At one end of the manor is a water mill, and at the other a windmill.

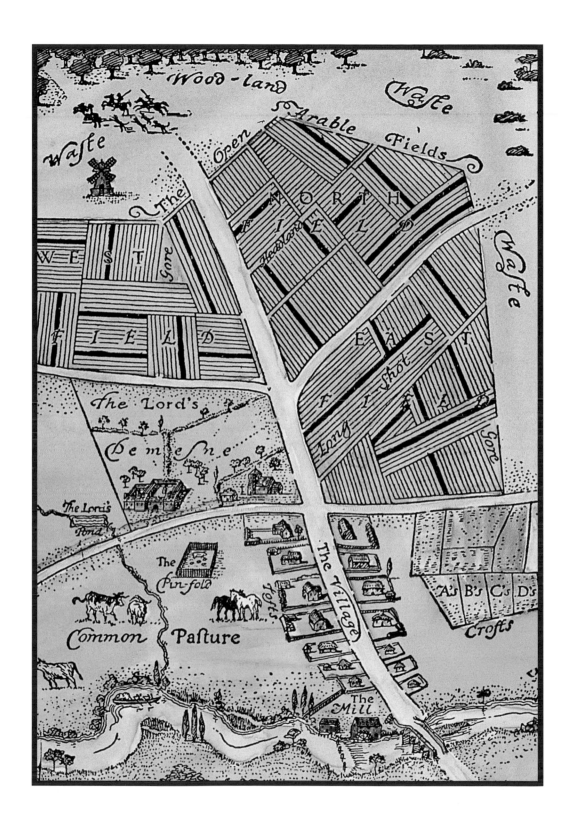

Wood-land

Waste

Waste

Arable Fields

The Gore

Open

NORTH FIELD

Headland

WEST FIELD

Waste

EAST FIELD

Long Ishot

Gore

The Lord's

Demesne

The Lord's Pond

The Pin-fold

Tofts

The Village

A's B's C's D's

Crofts

Common Pasture

The Mill

"A MESS OF POTTAGE"

Pottage was a meal-in-a-bowl, a combination of grain, vegetables, and, sometimes, a little meat. During the Middle Ages English villagers ate pottage nearly every day. Similar soups and stews were common fare for peasants in the rest of Europe, too. You may enjoy making your own version of this medieval dish.

Basic Ingredients

 sprouted barley grains, boiled with:
 peas and/or broad beans (fava beans)
 a little salted pork or bacon (the medieval peasant would not
  have had this very often)
 chopped onion
 crushed garlic

Add, depending on availability and personal taste (medieval peasants tended to add anything that grew, so long as it wasn't poisonous!):

 chopped or shredded cabbage
 chopped leeks
 diced turnip and/or parsnip
 strawberry, primrose, and/or violet leaves (in early spring)
 chopped hazelnuts (filberts) and/or walnuts
 diced apples and/or pears
 pitted (possibly dried) cherries
 chervil, savory, and/or thyme to season

Note: Pepper would taste very good in this recipe, but in the Middle Ages pepper was a luxury item that most peasants couldn't afford.

Shepherds lead a flock of sheep out to pasture while women milk cows and churn butter. Artist Simon Bening painted this farmyard scene around the year 1515.

a few windows, which had shutters but no glass. In a typical long-house there was a central hearth, where a fire burned all day long. A pot of porridge or pottage, a thick hearty stew, usually could be found simmering over it. Since there was often no real chimney, the inside of the house was not only dim, but also smoky.

Most families had little furniture. They ate meals at a trestle table—a board laid over supports—which was taken down every night. They sat on stools or benches. Instead of beds, most peasants slept on thin, straw-filled mattresses on the floor, sometimes in a loft at one end of the hall. Wooden chests were used to store blankets and clothes.

There was no bathroom, and no indoor plumbing at all. Usually one or two wells served the entire village. Women and children had to fetch water from the well every day. Like most medieval Europeans, peasants bathed very rarely. When they did, their bathtub was a barrel with the top removed. Family members washed up one after the other, all using the same water. For other bathroom needs, most people simply went "a bowshot away" from the house, although some families dug a latrine trench in the yard.

PUBLIC PLACES

Along with the private houses, every village had some buildings that served the entire community. The church and the manor house were the most important of these.

The village church was usually a simple stone building. There were no benches or pews—worshipers had to sit on the floor, stand, or bring stools from home. Fancy stained glass windows were probably rare in village churches, but the inside walls were often painted with biblical scenes. A favorite scene was the Last Judgment, showing God deciding who would be eternally rewarded and who would be eternally punished at the end of time.

Just outside was the churchyard, which included the village cemetery. Villagers often held dances and other festivities in the churchyard. Many priests disapproved of this, but some joined right in.

Normally a village would have only one church (although some had none). But if the village was part of more than one manor, it would probably have more than one manor house. Like the church, the manor house was built of stone, but it was much larger. It stood on an acre or two of ground and was often surrounded by a

The great hall of Castle Hedingham, built in England around 1130. The great hall of a manor house would have been very similar, though perhaps a bit smaller.

WIND AND WATER

Grain was the basis of the peasant diet. It could be boiled to make porridge and gruel, or ground into flour to make bread. In northern Europe before the Middle Ages, grain was usually ground in stone querns, or hand mills. The ancient Romans generally used large millstones turned by donkeys or slaves. Yet the Romans knew of a better technology: the waterwheel, which probably originated in Persia or India. Mysteriously, the Romans rarely used the waterwheel.

In the early Middle Ages, however, western Europeans realized the great potential of the waterwheel. By the eleventh century, water-powered mills were grinding grain into flour all over Europe—wherever there was a fast-running stream to turn the mill's waterwheel. The wheel turned a pair of gears, which turned the millstone. Large amounts of grain could now be ground with very little effort.

Toward the end of the twelfth century, a new European invention made still more progress in the technology of grinding grain. This was the vertical windmill, probably developed in eastern England. Nothing like it had ever been seen before, but it was soon in use throughout western Europe. It caught the force of the wind in its sails, and their turning ran the gears that turned the millstone, grinding grain with little human effort.

The waterwheel and the windmill are examples of medieval Europe's search for new forms of nonhuman power and new ways to use it. Such technological advances pointed the way to even greater progress in the future.

Women carry sacks of grain to the mill. The waterwheel, which turns the millstone to grind the grain, is clearly seen in the background.

wall, fence, or moat. Within this enclosure there were also likely to be stables, barns, sheepfolds, dovecotes, a chapel, a garden and orchard, a dairy, a kitchen, and a bakehouse.

The bailiff and his family lived in the manor house. This was also the place where royal messengers, high-ranking churchmen, friends and relatives of the lord, and other VIPs stayed when they visited the estate.

The most important feature of the manor house was the great hall, a huge, long, high-ceilinged room. Here guests were entertained, holidays were celebrated, and meetings were held. Above all, this was where the manorial court met.

Other community buildings might include one or more mills, where grain was ground into flour; ovens or bake houses; and a forge, where a blacksmith made horseshoes and iron tools. In many places there was a village green. Often it was not big enough for livestock to graze on. In the village of Elton, in eastern England, the village green seems to have been used mainly as the site where some lawbreakers were publicly punished.

4

THE VILLAGERS

In the Middle Ages, an average village had from 150 to 250 residents. In Scandinavia and some other places, however, peasants tended to live on separate, scattered farmsteads rather than in villages. Even among villages there were differences. By the High Middle Ages, many European villages were independent from manors. In England, however, the manorial system continued to have great power, and many of the surviving records about medieval peasant life come from the English manors.

Most of the peasants on a manor were tenants who rented their land from the lord. But although they were tenants, they felt very strongly that the land they held belonged to them. Lords recognized this (in fact, they usually felt the same way about the lands granted them by their own overlords) and respected it. When a man died, his land holding passed to one of his sons, usually the oldest. In some places the land was divided up among all the sons, or shared by all the sons. If a man had no sons, in most areas a daughter could inherit. Whatever the arrangement, the important thing was to keep the land in the family.

In some areas peasant allods were very common. An allod was a freeholding, land that no lord had any claim on. There were parts of Europe where it was possible for peasants to own allods at the

Magpies watch two peasants slaughtering a pig while other peasants work in the bake house and wash house on the lord's demesne.

same time as they held land from a lord. In other places allods were nonexistent.

DEGREES OF FREEDOM

Peasants were legally categorized as either unfree or free. These categories had to do with how much service was owed to the lord. Some manors had few if any free peasants. In the late thirteenth century the English village of Elton had twenty-two free households

A villein from the French countryside

and forty-eight unfree households (and twenty-eight others that were unclassified).

The unfree were known as serfs or villeins (vih-LANES). They were required to work the lord's land or perform other work a certain number of days each week. The more land a villein held, the more labor he or she had to do. By the thirteenth century, however, many lords were accepting money instead of work from their serfs. (The work still needed to be done, however, so the villeins' payments would be used to hire laborers for the demesne.)

Serfs also owed the lord numerous fees, which varied from manor to manor. In general, there was an annual payment known as head money, which symbolized the serfs' bond to their lord. The lord could demand a tax known as tallage whenever he had need of extra cash. When an unfree woman married, she, her father, or her husband had to pay the lord a fee called merchet. If her husband did not live on one of the lord's manors, an extra fine was added to this. Another fee was paid if a serf moved off the manor (this was supposed to be paid every year after the serf left). When a villein died, the lord had to be given the family's best cow or sheep; sometimes the lord took a piece of furniture or other household item instead. There was still another payment when a serf took over a landholding, whether he bought or inherited it. Serfs who wanted to become priests, monks, or nuns could not do so unless they paid a fine to the lord. Villeins also had to turn over agricultural products at particular times of year—for example, a certain number of chickens, eggs, or cakes of beeswax at Christmas and Easter.

Unfree peasants were required to grind their grain at the lord's mill; the miller kept a portion of the flour for the lord, as well as a portion for himself. This was so hateful to many peasants that they hid hand mills in their houses and secretly ground their own grain.

Once the serfs had flour, they could bake their bread only in the lord's ovens. Again, many simply didn't eat bread, but instead boiled their grain into porridge. Villeins were also frequently required to keep their sheep in the lord's sheepfold for the winter—the lord then had all of the sheeps' manure to fertilize the demesne, while the serfs had little fertilizer for their own fields.

Both free and unfree peasants paid the lord some form of rent for their land. Otherwise, free peasants owed the lord little labor and were exempt from all the fines and fees imposed on villeins. On the other hand, in most parts of Europe by the twelfth century, even a manor's free tenants were expected to be obedient to the lord, and they looked to him for protection just as the serfs did. A free peasant who moved off the manor, however, was no longer tied to its lord in any way, while villeins were bound to their lord no matter where they went, usually for as long as they lived.

Not surprisingly, no one wanted the burdens and obligations of being a serf. We have many records of villeins going to court to try to prove that they were actually free; they almost never succeeded. There were other ways, however, to achieve freedom. In many places the serf who moved to a town and lived there for a year and a day was automatically free. During the twelfth and thirteenth centuries, peasants in England, France, Spain, and especially Germany were encouraged to settle in new areas and found new villages. They cleared forests and drained marshes to create farmland where there had never been any before. In return, these colonists were guaranteed freedom for themselves and their descendants. During the High Middle Ages, lords also became increasingly willing to allow serfs to buy their freedom.

HALF A WORLD AWAY . . .
VILLAGE LIFE AMONG THE INCA

The thirteenth century saw the manorial system flourishing in England and other parts of Europe. Halfway around the world, in what is now Peru, the Incas were beginning their rise to power. Eventually the Incas ruled a huge empire, based largely on highly organized agriculture. As in medieval Europe, most of the people in this empire were peasant farmers.

In theory, all Inca lands belonged to the emperor. Each area's farmland was divided into three parts: one for the Sun, one for the emperor, and one for the local community. The peasants were required to work all three, and they could tend their own fields only after tending the Sun's and the emperor's. The lands of the Sun provided food for all of the empire's many priests and priestesses. The crops grown on the emperor's lands fed the royal family, the nobles, and government officials. The local community's land was divided up by the area's chief each autumn. Every married man received enough land to support his family.

Peasant men were required to perform regular labor services for the Inca government. These services included such things as working in mines, working as servants to the nobles, transporting goods from place to place, and participating in all kinds of building projects. Some communities had to provide feathers, fish, seashells, wood, and other raw materials to the emperor and nobles. In addition, every peasant was expected to weave one garment a year for the government storehouses; this weaving was usually done by the women. Sometimes a wife also accompanied her husband and helped him in various ways when he went away on his work assignment.

PEASANTS HIGH AND LOW

Whether villagers were free or not, they generally fit into one of three classes. At the top of village society were the wealthiest peasants, who were always few in number. These people held between forty and one hundred acres of land, some of which they rented to their own tenants. In some places, such as Germany, one of these wealthier peasants might occasionally rise into the lower nobility. On the other hand, members of the lower nobility occasionally sank into this peasant class.

The largest group of peasants was made up of those who held twelve to thirty-two acres. Twelve acres of land was just enough to support the average peasant family, at least in a good year. With thirty-two acres, the family would have surplus crops to sell.

The lowest class held no land at all, or too little to support a family. Cotters were peasants who had only a cottage and yard, or at most an acre or so. Most cotters and other peasants with little land worked as laborers for the lord or for other peasants. Some landless villagers, however, were able to make a living by practicing various crafts.

A village might have a number of craftspeople or tradespeople, such as blacksmiths, carpenters, shoemakers, weavers, dyers, tanners, millers, and butchers. These people were very important to the life of the village. They could be free or unfree, and some might practice their trades along with farming. Many women brewed and sold ale, and nearly all women did spinning, weaving, and sewing. Most of this cloth making was done for the family, but sometimes women did earn wages for this work. Women also served the village as midwives and healers.

Besides the farmers and craftspeople, there were other residents of the typical village. The lord's desmesne had a staff that included servants, plowmen, shepherds, a cook, a dairyman or dairymaid, and others. These people were often settled on small holdings on the demesne. The parish priest and his assistants lived on land near the church. Finally, on the fringes of village society there were various "strangers," for example traveling craftspeople (such as tinkers) and wandering beggars. Villagers tended to be very suspicious of these strangers. Sometimes a villager could be fined for hiring strangers or giving them food or shelter.

5

WORK, WORK, WORK

The medieval peasant's life revolved around the work of raising crops and livestock. Even most of the village craftspeople who didn't do farmwork earned their livings by either making agricultural tools (such as plowshares and hoes) or processing agricultural products (such as grain and leather).

The greatest events of the work year were plowing, planting, and harvesting. These were all community efforts, carried out by all of the villagers at the same time. The way these tasks were done was strictly regulated by the village bylaws, which were made by the villagers themselves. For example, in Elton, "strangers" who were hired to help with the harvest were not allowed to carry any of the grain.

Plowing was done in both spring and fall to prepare the fields for planting. The fallow field was plowed in summer to keep down weeds. In a typical family, the husband guided the plow and his wife goaded the horses or oxen who pulled it. (Most peasants could not afford to keep enough horses or oxen to pull a plow, so families combined their resources, sharing both animals and plows.) After planting, the grain fields had to be weeded frequently. When harvest time came, every able-bodied person in the village took part in cutting, binding, and carting or carrying the sheaves of grain.

Historians used to think that nearly all outdoor, agricultural work was done by men, while women worked in the fields only

Sheepshearing was usually done in the month of June.

A plow team at work. One man steers the plow while the other goads the oxen who are pulling it.

at harvest. Recent studies have shown that women, and girls, did a great deal more. They hauled manure to fertilize the fields, sowed seed, hoed, weeded, separated wheat from chaff, took part in haymaking, and carried grain to the mill. In regions where grape growing was important, women worked alongside men in the vineyards, pruning and tying vines. In some areas, such as southwestern France, all shepherds were men. But in many other places females tended not only sheep but also cows and oxen, geese and chickens, and pigs. Women's tasks included feeding, milking, shearing, and slaughtering the livestock in their care.

In peasant families all household work was done by women and girls. They tended the hearth fire and carried water from the well. They spun and dyed wool, wove cloth, and made the clothes for everyone in the household. They raised vegetables in the croft and prepared all the family's meals. Other responsibilities included making butter and cheese, and preserving food for the winter. If a

ENDLESSLY SPINNING

From ancient times through the Middle Ages, spinning was a woman's common chore. Its tools were very simple: the distaff, basically a long forked stick; and the spindle, a short, thin stick with a round weight on the bottom. The unspun wool was wound around the distaff, which the spinner held in her left hand (the "distaff side"—a phrase that has also come to mean the mother's side of the family). With her right hand the spinner drew out the wool fibers and meshed their ends with thread that was already on the spindle. Then she gave the spindle a twist to set it spinning. As it spiraled down to the ground, the spindle's motion stretched and twisted the wool, making a strong thread. When the thread was long enough, the spinner paused to wind it around the spindle, then drew out more wool and began again.

With distaff and spindle, women could take their spinning everywhere, and they usually did. They spun not only while they were relaxing around the hearth fire in the evenings, but also while they were engaged in other tasks in the yard and fields. In fact, they spun whenever their hands were not busy with something else. This was essential, because it took a great deal of thread to weave enough cloth to make clothes for the entire family. (Not surprisingly, most peasants got only one or two new outfits a year!)

In the late thirteenth century, a new invention came on the scene in Europe. This was the spinning wheel, which may have originated in India or the Middle East. It took half as much time to spin thread on a spinning wheel as it did to spin the same amount of thread with a drop spindle. However, many years passed before the new invention was widely adopted, especially in the countryside. Hand spinning wool produced better quality thread than spinning with a wheel. Spinning wheels were expensive, too, and they could not be carried everywhere. So for several centuries more, most peasant women continued to spin the old-fashioned way.

family was able to raise any extra food, it was often the wife who went to a market or fair to sell the surplus.

In most places peasant women could legally both buy and inherit land. In one part of England in the fourteenth century, 14 percent of the peasant landholders were women, most of them

This illustration from an Italian manuscript shows a peasant woman selling eggs and roosters at a market.

widows. All women landholders, free and unfree, were required to work their holdings and owed the lord the same rents and services as male landholders. We have records of many independent peasant women. One, for example, left her home village in south-western France and bought a house, farm, and vineyard in another village. She kept a flock of sheep and dyed their wool to earn money. During harvest time she and her children worked as hired laborers.

6
FAMILY LIFE

In the Middle Ages, nobles often did not have very strong family ties. Men were frequently away at war, perhaps for years at a time, and women rarely nursed their own babies. Children of great lords were likely to be raised mainly by servants.

Peasant families, on the other hand, tended to be quite close. Children spent most of their time with their parents. And every family member had an important role to play in ensuring the household's survival.

The peasant household typically included parents, children, and sometimes a few other relatives—usually a widowed parent or an unmarried sibling of the husband or wife. Wealthier households might also have a couple of servants.

Well-off peasant families generally had an average of five children. Poorer families were likely to have only two or three. Most households had a cat, to keep down rodents, and perhaps a dog or two, to guard the home and livestock. (In southern France, however, peasants tended to be highly suspicious of cats, regarding them as creatures of the devil.) These animals may often have been treated with affection, but most people probably thought of their cats and dogs more as working farm animals than as pets.

A mother-to-be braces herself against the pains of labor. She is lucky to have a midwife helping her.

A MEDIEVAL CHILDHOOD

All babies were born at home. Birth was a frightening and dangerous experience because there were not many medical techniques to help out if something went wrong. Also, no one in medieval Europe knew about germs, so no measures were taken to prevent infection. During labor the mother-to-be was supported and comforted by two or three women friends and relatives. If she was lucky, an experienced midwife would also be there to help deliver the baby. But even with a midwife's care, many mothers and babies died either during or soon after birth.

If the baby lived, it was promptly baptized in order to bring it into the Christian faith. (The mother did not attend the baptism; she was not allowed into the church for some weeks and had to go through a ceremony of purification first.) If the mother lived, she normally breast-fed the child herself for one to two years. Otherwise another village woman would have to nurse and care for the child. In real emergencies, peasants sometimes made a kind of baby bottle out of a cow's horn.

Medieval peasants did not get maternity or parental leave. Very soon after birth, the mother had to return to work. She might carry the baby with her in a slinglike device as she went about her tasks, or she might have one of her older children or an elderly villager look after the baby. Single mothers seem to have had the most difficult time arranging childcare. One mother in southwestern France, who worked as a servant and laborer, had another village woman care for her daughter. When the mother switched jobs, she also sought out a new caregiver, who lived closer to her new job.

Unfortunately, parents sometimes had to leave young children unattended, often with tragic results. Many records have survived that tell of children dying in house fires, falling into wells and ponds, and being injured or killed in other accidents. Children were also highly vulnerable to disease, and many died before reaching their teens.

Some historians have said that because death in childhood was so common, medieval parents did not let themselves become very attached to their children. However, many sources now show that peasants, at least, were by-and-large devoted parents. When a child died, whether from disease or an accident, the parents might grieve for a very long time. Sometimes they would even name their next child after the one who had died, hoping that in this way the dead child would be "remade."

Childhood was brief, however, and most peasant children had few, if any, toys. They played imaginatively with flowers, sticks, bits of wood, pieces of cloth, and the like. For example, a medieval sermon describes a child making a "sailing ship" out of a crust of bread and building a "great hall" with pieces of wood. A cloth decorated with flowers could be a lovely lady, and a long stick made a fine white horse.

As soon as they were old enough, children began to work, helping with their parents' daily tasks. By the age of twelve they were doing adult work, even plowing. They labored not only on the family's land but also, if they were serfs, on the demesne. (If the mother was a serf, the child was automatically a serf, too.)

For most peasant children, following and helping their parents was their only form of education, and it was all they would ever need. A few boys became apprentices (students being trained in a craft) to a carpenter, smith, or other craftsman, either at home or in a nearby town. In some villages the parish priest ran a small school for peasant boys. They probably learned little more than the basics of reading, writing, arithmetic, and religion. This would be enough, though, to help them if they ever became a reeve, beadle, or other manorial official. The parish schools were also preparation for boys who eventually became parish priests themselves. In the south of France boys from wealthy peasant families were able to get university educations from time to time. Also in southern France, there were some religious groups who taught poor girls to read. Otherwise, however, peasant girls seem to have had no opportunities for any kind of schooling.

A carpenter works in his shop while his wife spins and their son gathers wood shavings from the floor.

FOR BETTER OR WORSE

Nearly all peasant girls married. Those who did not worked as servants and hired laborers, often on the demesne, or they might live with a married brother and help his family with both housework and farmwork. Sometimes unmarried women left the village and went to work on another manor or in a town.

Girls could legally marry at the age of twelve. Usually, however, peasant brides were between fifteen and twenty years old. Peasant men were typically in their mid to late twenties when they married.

Most marriages were arranged by the families of the couple. Sometimes the groom-to-be would start this process—if he liked a certain girl, he might ask his parents to try to arrange for him to marry her. When the families were well-off, there might be long negotiations. The bride had to have a dowry of money, goods, or farm animals to bring to the marriage. The groom had to guarantee a dower, the portion of his property that would be his wife's if he died before she did. If the families were villeins, it was important to decide who would pay merchet to the lord.

Once everyone was satisfied, the couple became betrothed, or engaged. Since villages were small, the two usually already knew each other (noble couples often had never met before their wedding). Parents could not force their children to marry. Both the bride and the groom had to agree to the marriage for it to be legal.

Peasant weddings were very informal. Often the couple simply exchanged promises and a kiss in front of the church door. Sometimes they would then go into the church to hear Mass. After the ceremony there would be a wedding feast to celebrate the new marriage. Some peasants, especially poor ones, were married even more simply, in what was called a private marriage. The couple made their wedding vows to each other with no priest, friends, or family members present to witness. But even though such a marriage began in secret, the couple was looked upon as being legally and truly married.

The newlyweds might move into a home of their own, or they might live, at least for a while, with one of their families. If they lived

A peasants' wedding celebration, painted in 1568 by the great Flemish artist Pieter Brueghel the Elder. The musicians are playing bagpipes, which were popular instruments among peasants throughout Europe during the Middle Ages and the Renaissance.

on a holding belonging to the woman or her family, the husband often took his wife's last name. Even so, the husband was always regarded as the head of the family. Nearly all medieval thinkers, writers, and preachers agreed that men were superior to women. Villagers heard this viewpoint everywhere, from sermons to jokes. Husbands were entitled to discipline their wives by hitting and even beating them. Women were expected to bear this treatment without complaining.

If a marriage was unhappy, peasant couples often separated. Sometimes they went through the process of getting a divorce, but sometimes they didn't bother, even if they wanted to remarry later. The second wedding might take place privately, or there might be a church-door ceremony in a neighboring village. As far as we know, none of this was particularly scandalous to medieval peasants.

VILLAGE ELDERS

One way or another, many peasant marriages ended up being full of affection and satisfaction for both partners. But marriage still did not last especially long. The average medieval peasant could expect to live for only about another twenty years after getting married. Since husbands were usually ten or so years older than their wives, a large number of women became widows. A widow was free to remain unmarried if she wished, although her family or lord might try to pressure her into remarriage. If she held land, she owed the lord all the rents and services due on it. If she did not remarry, she either had to work the land herself or hire laborers to work it for her.

People were considered to be elderly when they reached age forty-five. In some places their age made them more respected in their families and in the village, but in other places the elderly were less respected. In southwestern France elderly women were held in high esteem and asked for advice on a regular basis. On the other hand, in northern Italy people feared that an old woman's "evil eye" could harm babies.

A villager who was too old to continue working generally transferred his or her holdings to the person who would inherit the land (usually a son). In return, the heir promised to support the "retiree." Some aging peasants made arrangements with other villagers to support them. Another possibility was to buy a kind of pension plan from a monastery. This provided a room, food, drink, clothing, candles, firewood, and even, if the peasant could afford it, servants and a house with a garden and pasture.

When a villager was very ill, the priest was summoned to help him or her prepare for death. Two things were of the greatest importance to peasants on their deathbed: to be surrounded by their loved ones, and to be assured that their souls were saved. After a person died, there was usually a day or two of keeping vigil over the body; these wakes often became merry, drunken parties. The body was washed and prepared for burial by the women of the family or neighborhood. In southwestern France, when the head of the household died, the family would keep some of his hair and fingernail clippings so that his good fortune would not desert the house.

Funerals were generally very simple. The body was sewn into or wrapped in a shroud, then laid on a bier and carried into the parish church. After Mass was said, the body was buried in the churchyard. Here, most medieval peasants believed, the dead person slept and awaited the Last Judgment.

7

REST AND RECREATION

In the Middle Ages, the average person thought of time very differently than we do. Peasants had no clocks or calendars. They were aware of the passing of the seasons and the phases of the moon, but they rarely thought in terms of hours, weeks, or months. They thought in terms of lunchtime, dinnertime, the amount of time it took to travel to the next village, and so on. Instead of months they would speak of "the season when the elm leaves appear" or "the time of the turnip harvest." They also described dates in terms of various Christian feast days: for example, the Nativity of the Virgin (September 8), All Souls' Day (November 2), the Feast of Saint John (June 24). In fact, almost every day of the year was dedicated to a saint, an event in the life of Jesus, or an important religious concept. Usually the parish priest had a calendar, and he would tell villagers when important days were.

Dutch artist Hieronymus Bosch, who lived from around 1450 to 1516, painted this scene of a magician amazing a crowd with his sleight-of-hand tricks. Peasants might see such an entertainer when they went into a town for market day, and sometimes traveling entertainers came to the villages.

TIME TO CELEBRATE!

Each season had at least one holiday when no work was done and the villagers were free to play games and feast. The greatest of all holidays was Christmas. Its celebrations lasted for twelve days. There were no Christmas trees, but people of all classes decorated their homes with holly, mistletoe, and other evergreens. On the manors, peasants owed the lord extra bread, eggs, and chickens. In some places a few or all of the villagers were invited to a Christmas feast in the great hall of the manor house.

BEE IN THE MIDDLE
A MEDIEVAL GAME

Bee in the Middle was a game often played during medieval Christmas celebrations. It was enjoyed by both children and adults. You might like to try it.

To play Bee in the Middle, the players need to sit in a circle on the floor. One player, the Bee, kneels or sits crosslegged in the middle of the circle. The Bee can lean forward, back, or side to side, but may not change position or get up. The other players try to touch the Bee, and the Bee tries to "sting" each toucher by grabbing his or her hand. This is a challenge, because the other players do not take their turns in any particular order. Although they go one at a time, they may surprise the Bee from any direction at any moment. Once the Bee manages to "sting" a toucher, that person becomes the Bee. The game can continue for as long as the players wish. Careful not to get too rough!

Beehives were a common sight in the medieval countryside. They were generally woven of wicker or straw, like this one.

Since Jesus was born among animals in a stable, farm animals were often honored during the Christmas season. The first serving of some of the special Christmas foods was given to a favorite horse or cow, and then all the animals received extra helpings of their usual feed. Besides commemorating the birth of Jesus, many peasants probably felt that their winter gift to the animals would help increase the strength and size of their herds and flocks in the spring.

The Christmas revels ended with Epiphany, or Twelfth Night (January 6). On this day country people in many areas took cups of cider and small cakes out to the fruit trees. They would walk or dance around the trees, singing something like this:

> *Hail to thee, old apple tree!*
> *From every bough*
> *Give us apples enow;*
> *Hatsful, capsful,*
> *Bushel, bushel, sacksful,*
> *And our arms full, too.*

Then there was another festive meal. In some English villages mummers, or amateur actors, would liven up the feast with traditional dances and plays. Often they acted out the story of Saint George and the dragon.

Easter week was celebrated with many games, often involving eggs (such as trying to roll an egg across the floor in a straight line). The lord of the manor usually received an extra payment of eggs from his tenants during this season. Once more, some villagers might be invited to feast at the manor house. The meal's main course was usually lamb or pork.

May Day was a joyous festival in much of northern and western Europe. It marked the beginning of summer and was celebrated with maypole dances and bonfires. On the eve of May Day, young people often stayed out in the woods all night. In the

SAINT GEORGE
AND THE DRAGON

During the Middle Ages, Saint George was one of the most widely honored Christian saints. He was said to have been a soldier who was born in Asia Minor during the late third century. A great many legends added to his story. In the most popular of these legends, Saint George went to Libya to fight a dragon. The dragon lived in a lake and had been gobbling down two sheep every day. When the area's villages ran out of sheep, the people offered the monster maidens to eat instead. No army had been able to destroy the dragon. However, Saint George was able to kill it with a single blow, just as the beast was about to devour a young princess. The king of the land gave the saint a huge reward for rescuing his daughter and delivering the people from the dragon's awful rampages. Saint George divided this reward among the poor villagers, then rode off on further adventures.

Villagers celebrate the feast of Saint George with dancing, wrestling matches, and mock combats. Pieter Brueghel the Younger (1564–1638) was the artist.

morning they returned to the village with flowers and green boughs to decorate their homes. Often one of the village girls was crowned with a wreath of flowers and named Queen of the May. Games and sports were played throughout the day, and the Queen of the May gave the winners their prizes.

In much of the British Isles, Lammas (August 1) was another occasion when villagers feasted at the manor house. This holiday celebrated harvest time. In some places villagers would "sing the harvest home," all gathering for a songfest in the manor's great hall. At this time, too, loaves of bread and other farm products were offered and blessed in church.

There were many other holidays and Christian feast days. In addition, each village celebrated an annual feast in honor of the parish's patron saint. Many villagers would stay up, keeping a vigil, all through the night before this day. In the morning they would go to hear a mass especially in honor of their patron. For the rest of the day there would be singing, dancing, storytelling, games, and wrestling matches, all frequently taking place in the churchyard.

THE DAY OF REST

As on major holidays, the villagers were excused from work on Sundays. Three church services were held on this day of rest, but most peasants went only to the midday Mass. Priests complained that it was often difficult to get people to attend church services at all. In fact, in some areas it was common for fewer than half the villagers to go to church regularly.

Mass was recited or sung by the priest. The words were in Latin, the official language of the Catholic church. Few if any peasants understood Latin, and there was little congregational participation in

"I HAVE A YOUNG SISTER,"
SONG FROM MEDIEVAL ENGLAND

The words of this song were first written down in the 1400s. It was so popular that it was eventually brought to North America by English settlers, and versions of it are still sung today.

I have a young sister
Far beyond the sea;
Many are the gifts
That she has sent to me.

She sent me a cherry
Without any stone,
And also sent a dove
Without any bone.

She sent me a briar
Without any sting;
She bade me love my sweetheart
Without longing.

How can any cherry
Be without a stone?
And how can any dove
Be without a bone?

How can any briar
Be without a sting?
How can I love my sweetheart
Without longing?

When the cherry was a flower,
Then it had no stone;
When the dove was an egg,
Then it had no bone.

When the briar was a seed,
Then it had no sting;
When a maiden has her sweetheart,
She has no more longing.

the worship service. People often got restless and commonly chatted and flirted with one another during Mass. Some parish priests preached a sermon in the people's own language, at least once in a while. The sermon would explain biblical teachings, describe the lives of the saints, tell stories that illustrated Christian values, or urge the people to give up sinful practices (such as dancing in the churchyard!). Sometimes a wandering friar or monk would come to the village and preach a lively sermon either in the church or outdoors, generally attracting a large crowd.

PLEASANT PASTIMES

Even on workdays, peasants didn't always labor from sunup to sundown. Whether in the fields or around the house, there was often time to take a break and gossip with a friend. Villagers frequently got together for company and conversation at dinner-time. After dinner they might sit around the hearth fire and talk long into the night. As they discussed everything from religious beliefs to their neighbors' love lives, the women spun or sewed and the men mended tools. Some nights there would be singing and storytelling in addition to the pleasures of good conversation. Men and women alike also socialized in taverns. In most villages, the tavern was simply the home of someone who had recently brewed a batch of ale. (In France and Italy, the favorite drink was wine.)

Games and sports were popular with both children and adults. Peasants played checkers, chess, and dice, as well as games like blind man's buff. Wrestling, archery, and swimming were among the favorite sports. Many people liked to watch cock fights, dog fights, and the like.

Sometimes traveling jugglers, musicians, storytellers, and other entertainers would come to a village. Along with the enjoyment they gave, they brought news and gossip from other areas.

HEROES OF SONG AND STORY

In the centuries before radio, television, and DVDs, storytelling was one of the most popular forms of entertainment. Some stories were in rhyme and set to music; these were called ballads. Peasants usually had to tell their own stories and sing their own ballads. Their opportunities to hear professional entertainers were rare.

Many peasant stories were like the Grimms' fairy tales that are read to children today. The medieval versions of such tales, however, tended to be much more violent and realistic than ours. They reflected the harsh realities of peasant life during that time. For example, in many of these stories, whenever the peasant heroes are offered any sort of magical gift or wish, all they want is food—good food, and plenty of it. To people who were often hungry and malnourished, hardly anything better could be imagined.

But peasants also liked to hear and tell stories about the great heroes of the past. In Ireland some of the most popular tales were about Fionn MacCumhal (Finn MacCool), the head of an ancient band of warriors. Fionn and his men encountered giants, fairies, sorcerers, and fierce enemies in their adventures. Only men were allowed to tell these tales, but everyone enjoyed hearing them.

Welsh peasants told of King Arthur and the group of heroes that gathered around him. These Arthurian stories spread to France and England and became incredibly popular all over Europe. French peasants also celebrated the deeds of Charlemagne, the ruler whose ninth-century empire stretched from France to central Europe. In northern Italy some medieval peasants even named their children after characters from the Charlemagne stories.

Peasants in Norway and Iceland told of their ancestors, the Viking raiders, explorers, and settlers of the ninth through eleventh centuries. They also enjoyed stories based on ancient legends about a dragon slayer, a warrior woman, and an enchanted ring. These tales were relished by German peasants, too.

From a manuscript of the early 1300s, a scene from a story about King Arthur and his knights. Arthur has been seriously wounded in battle and is near death. Knowing this, he has entrusted his sword Excalibur to his faithful knight Bedivere. Excalibur was given to Arthur long ago by the mysterious Lady of the Lake; now it must be returned to her. When Bedivere throws the sword into the lake, a woman's hand reaches up out of the water, catches the sword, and brandishes it aloft. Arthur's marvelous reign has come to an end.

The hero of many Spanish stories was El Cid. An eleventh-century military leader, El Cid fought both for and against the Muslims in Spain. He won renown not only for his bravery but also for his dedication to justice and his love for his wife and daughters.

Robin Hood, the most famous of all medieval peasant heroes, was not a warrior or king but an outlaw. He is still a popular character, but his legend has changed a great deal since medieval times. When his adventures were first celebrated in northern England and southern Scotland in the thirteenth century, Robin Hood was a well-known robber and enemy of the English king. During the next few centuries his reputation increased, until he became the noble thief, who stole from the rich to give to the poor, that we know so well today. And although Little John was an important character from the very beginning, Maid Marian did not become part of the Robin Hood legend until after the Middle Ages.

STRANGE AND SUNDRY LANDS

Travel, much more often than we might expect, was another way that people in the Middle Ages entertained themselves. Kings, along with their nobles and households, liked to make "progresses" through the countryside. Peasants went to fairs and markets in neighboring villages and towns. All sorts of people also went on pilgrimages, journeys to important religious sites. Pilgrimages were believed to be good for a person's soul, but they also provided an opportunity to see new places, meet new people, and experience new things.

"ROBIN HOOD AND THE MONK"

"Rhymes of Robin Hood" were popular with English peasants as early as the 1300s. The first of these rhymes to be written down, in 1450, was the ballad of "Robin Hood and the Monk." This is a story about Robin Hood's visit to a Nottingham church on the holy day of Whitsun, or Pentecost, and his subsequent arrest and escape from prison. The poem portrays Robin's devotion to the Virgin Mary as well as his daring and the faithfulness of his "merry men." Here, adapted into modern English, are some stanzas from this popular medieval ballad:

In summer, when the woods are bright,
And leaves are large and long,
It is full merry in the fair forest
To hear the sweet birds' song,

To see the deer draw to the dale
And leave the hills so high
And shade themselves beneath the leaves,
Under the greenwood tree.

So it befell upon Whitsun,
Early in a May morning,
The sun rose up shining fair,
And the merry birds did sing.

"A merry morning," said Little John,
"By Christ that died on the tree!
There is no man merrier than I
In all of Christianity.

"Pluck up your heart, my dear master,"
Little John did say,
"And think how fair a time it is
In a morning of May!"

"Yet one thing grieves me," said Robin,
"And does my heart much woe:
That I may not on this holy day
To mass or other service go.

"It is two weeks and more," said he,
"Since my Savior I have seen.
Today I will go to Nottingham,
With the might of the sweet Virgin."

Unfortunately, Robin and Little John quarrel, and so Robin goes off to Nottingham alone. While he is praying in church, a certain monk recognizes him and betrays him to the sheriff. After a short fight, Robin is arrested. But Little John is loyal still, and uses trickery and strength to set Robin free. Soon the pair of outlaws are safely back in their forest home:

The sheriff made to search Nottingham,
Through every street and alley,
But Robin was in merry Sherwood,
Lighthearted as leaf on tree.

. . .

Thus John got Robin Hood out of prison —
It is certain, without a doubt.
When his men saw him safe and sound,
With gladness they did shout.

They poured out wine to celebrate,
Under the leaves so small,
And ate pastries filled with venison,
And washed them down with ale.

CHAUCER'S PEASANT PILGRIMS

Geoffrey Chaucer, who lived from about 1340 to 1400, was one of the greatest writers in English literature. His most famous book is *The Canterbury Tales*, in which a group of people on a pilgrimage to the shrine of Thomas à Becket in Canterbury entertain one another by telling stories. Four of the pilgrims are typical country dwellers: the Parson, the Plowman, the Miller, and the Reeve. Here, adapted into modern English, are Chaucer's descriptions of each of them:

THE PARSON

There was a good man of religion,
A poor parson of a small town,
Who Christ's gospel truly preached.
His parishioners he would devoutly teach.
He was good-willed and wondrously diligent,
And in adversity always patient.

. . .

His parish was wide, with houses far asunder,
But he never failed, in rain or thunder,
In sickness or in trouble, to visit
The farthest parishioners, well-off and not,
Going all on foot, in his hand a staff.
This noble example to his sheep he gave:
First he acted, and afterward he taught.
Out of the Gospel these words he caught:
"If gold rusts, what can iron do?"
For if a priest is foul, in whom we trust,
No wonder if a common man should rust!

. . .

To draw folk to heaven by fairness
And good example—this was his business.

. . .

The teachings of Christ and of the Twelve
Were what he taught—but first he followed them himself.

THE PLOWMAN

With the parson there was a plowman, his brother,
Who had hauled many a cartload of manure.
A good and honest laborer was he,
Living in peace and perfect charity.
He loved God best with his whole heart
At all times, whether life was easy or hard,
And next he loved his neighbor as himself.
He would thresh and also dig and delve,
For Christ's sake, for every poor creature,
Without any pay, if it lay in his power.

Chaucer's pilgrims on their way to Canterbury

THE MILLER

The miller was a stout fellow for any occasion.
He was full big of muscle and also of bone:
That proved well, for everywhere he came
To wrestle, he would win the first-prize ram.
. . .
His beard was as broad as a digging spade.
Right on the tip of his nose he had
A wart, and upon it stood a tuft of hairs
As red as the bristles of a pig's ears.
His nostrils were black and wide.
He bore a sword and small shield at his side.
. . .
His mouth was as big as a wide furnace door.
He was a loud boaster and a rude joker—
His jests were of sin and ribaldry.
He could well steal grain, taking three times his fee—
He had a thumb of gold, by God.
He wore a white coat and a blue hood.

THE REEVE

The reeve was a slender man with a choleric mood.
He shaved his beard as close as he could.
. . .
Well could he keep a storehouse and a bin—
No auditor could do him in.
He knew by dry weather and by the rain
How well the seed would yield the grain.
His lord's sheep, his cattle, his dairy,

His pigs, his horse, his stock, and his poultry—
All were wholly in this reeve's governing,
And on his honor he gave the reckoning.
. . .

The Reeve

There was no bailiff, no herder or other soul,
Whose tricks and cheating he did not know;
They were in dread of him as they were of death.
His dwelling was full fair upon a heath.

. . .

He was rich with all that he had stored.
Subtly could he please his lord,
Making gifts and loans from the lord's own goods,
And receive thanks from him, with a coat and hood.
In youth he had apprenticed with a master
To become a good craftsman, a carpenter.

8

HARD TIMES

Like farmers everywhere throughout time, medieval peasants were at the mercy of the weather. Constant, heavy rains could delay planting, cause already-planted seed to mold in the ground, flood seedlings, or ruin an almost-ripe crop. If there was not enough rain during the growing season, the crops would dry up. Hailstorms and early frosts were especially dreaded threats as harvest time approached.

Time was also the peasant's enemy, especially the serf's. There were only so many days when conditions were right for plowing, planting, and harvesting. Villeins had to tend not only their own crops but also the lord's. In Elton, for most of the year the serfs were required to work for the lord two days a week. But in August the requirement increased to three days, and in September—at the height of the harvest—to five. This left little time for serfs to work their own land.

Peasant farmers were responsible for almost the entire food supply of medieval Europe. And yet peasants often had little to eat themselves. They frequently suffered from malnutrition. They ate meat rarely—sometimes only on major feast days—and had few other sources of protein. The variety of fruits and vegetables available to them might also be quite limited.

There were few effective cures for illnesses in the Middle Ages. Many people believed that "being bled" regularly would keep disease-causing substances from building up in their bodies.

During this period, there were not many effective treatments for disease. Peasants' health was also threatened by poor sanitation. Not only was there no indoor plumbing, but even outhouses seem to have been almost unheard of. And in some places, villagers commonly had huge piles of animal manure right in their yards.

The demands of the lord caused additional hardship for a great many peasants. The numerous rents, fines, and fees could be a crippling burden for the poor. Strict limits were placed on how much firewood peasants could gather from the forests, and hunting by peasants was usually forbidden. Even if wolves, deer, or other creatures came out of the woods and destroyed the flocks or crops of the villagers, they still were not allowed to shoot at the animals. Villeins who were injured or seriously ill were given sick leave for up to a year, but after that they were required to return to work whether they were well or not. There were always some peasants who ended up wandering from village to village, unable to support themselves except by begging.

PLAGUE AND PILLAGE

In the fourteenth century a series of disasters added to the routine hardships of peasant life. First came two years of extremely bad harvests, which led to widespread starvation. In England this was followed by epidemics of typhoid fever and livestock diseases. But the worst was yet to come.

In 1347–1350 the Black Death, a devastating plague, swept through Europe. Rich and poor; young and old; cities, castles, villages, monasteries—none could escape the disease, but children

A priest helps a victim of the plague prepare for death. The attendants wear hoods and masks in hopes of protecting themselves from the dread disease.

and the poor were most vulnerable. Many areas lost one-third to two-thirds of their people. After this first outbreak, the plague struck six more times before 1420.

At the same time, the Hundred Years' War was raging between England and France. Peasants bore the burden of the higher and more frequent taxes imposed by the kings of both countries. Peasants were also drafted to fight in the armies. The war was waged entirely in France, so French villagers suffered worst of all. Their homes, crops, and lives were threatened not only by the invading English soldiers, but also by bands of French soldiers raiding for supplies.

Depopulation and heavy taxation severely weakened numerous villages, where holdings and houses stood empty for years. Land was now cheap, but labor was expensive. Prices for food and other necessities climbed dramatically. Peasants demanded higher pay, and lords demanded higher rents and fees. Due to labor shortages, laws were passed to try to force peasants to remain on the manors and work, at whatever jobs they were ordered to, at the lower wages of the past.

Peasant uprisings had occurred from time to time since the early Middle Ages. But in the second half of the fourteenth century, a spirit of rebellion seemed to explode all over Europe. There were peasant revolts in France, Flanders (modern Belgium), England, Germany, Spain, and Italy. The most famous of these uprisings was the English Peasants' War, or Wat Tyler's Rebellion, of 1381. The

Wat Tyler, leader of a rebellion against serfdom, is killed by the Lord Mayor of London as King Richard II looks on. The execution put an end to the English Peasants' War of 1381.

English rebels succeeded in entering London and presenting their demands to the king, Richard II. This revolt, however, like all the others, was ultimately crushed.

Nevertheless, a turning point had been reached. In most of Europe, the time was soon coming when serfdom and obligations to the lord of the manor would be things of the past. In a couple more centuries, European peasants would begin to take their way of life across the Atlantic Ocean to the New World. We are fortunate that in small towns throughout Europe and North America, the medieval village's spirit of community and cooperation lives on.

THE CHURCH

1
THE MAKING OF CHRISTENDOM

In the year 313 Constantine I was the emperor of Rome. Roman rule stretched from Spain to the Middle East, taking in most of western Europe and all of southern Europe. Throughout the empire, people practiced many different religions, including a fairly new one, Christianity. At this time, only about 10 percent of western Europe's people were Christians, and Christianity had a much lower status than most other religions. But Constantine had been learning a great deal about the new faith, and he came to a momentous decision: he would give Christianity equal rights and privileges with other religions. Most of the emperors who came after Constantine were Christians, and they continued to strengthen the Church. By the year 400 Christianity was the official religion of the empire.

Beyond the empire's boundaries, among the people whom the Romans called barbarians, ancient religions still flourished. The Church, however, believed it had a duty to bring all people into the Christian faith. Since Christianity's beginnings, missionaries had traveled far and wide to spread their religion. Now, with the support and protection of the government, the Church could send out even more missionaries and spread Christianity even farther.

Charlemagne oversees the building of a new church at his capital city in France.

In the late 400s, the western half of the Roman Empire fell to barbarian invaders. The Church remained strong, however, and eventually the invaders converted to Christianity. One Christian descendant of the barbarians was Charles Martel, who turned away a new set of invaders in 732. These were Muslim warriors, who for a hundred years had been carrying their religion, Islam, from its homeland in Arabia. They had conquered North Africa and advanced up through Spain, but Martel stopped them from going farther into Europe. He became a hero to Christian Europe and founded a line of powerful rulers.

Charles Martel's grandson Charlemagne built a new empire that stretched from France to central Europe. In the year 800 the pope, head of the Church, crowned Charlemagne emperor of Rome. Charlemagne's empire did not last long after his death, but the idea of Europe unified by the Church endured throughout the Middle Ages. The Christian nations of Europe thought of themselves as belonging to the religious realm known as Christendom.

Missionaries continued to spread Christianity to places as far away as Iceland in the west and Russia in the east. Meanwhile, the eastern half of the old Roman Empire was flourishing as the Byzantine Empire. Its culture differed from that of western Europe in many ways. In particular, the Byzantine churches had serious disagreements with some of the practices and beliefs of the western European churches. In 1054 Christianity split into two factions, which eventually came to be known as the Roman Catholic Church in the West and the Orthodox Church in the East. By 1300 Catholic Christianity was the official religion of nearly every country in western Europe.

NON-CHRISTIAN EUROPE

Many people tend to think that all medieval Europeans were Christians. This is not true, however. Several ancient European religions survived well into the Middle Ages. The people of Sweden, for example, still had a temple to the old gods Thor, Odin, and Frey in the twelfth century. Even after the Swedish king declared Christianity his country's official religion, and even after the last temple was closed, country people kept to their traditional beliefs for decades (perhaps even centuries) more. Across the Baltic Sea from Sweden, old ways held on even longer—the last northern European state to become officially Christian was Lithuania, in 1386.

European peoples nearly always converted to Christianity "from the top down." First the king would decide to become a Christian, and his nobles would gradually follow his example. With the ruling class's support, the Church was then able to start establishing parishes—local or neighborhood churches—throughout the country. Over time, the average people would adopt Christian beliefs. This was not always a peaceful process, however. The Church banned many traditional practices and often harassed people who followed them. Threats and violence were frequently used to force people to accept the new religion.

While ancient, traditional religions held on in northern Europe, southern Europe felt the strong presence of Islam. The kingdom of Granada, in southern Spain, was a Muslim nation until 1492. Many parts of southeastern Europe also became officially Muslim in the mid-1300s. During this period, the Ottoman Empire was expanding from its lands in Turkey, taking Islam with it to all the areas it conquered. Muslim merchants and travelers also spent a great deal of time doing business in European cities such as Venice.

Medieval cities commonly had sizable Jewish populations. But Jews suffered from many prejudices and restrictions. However, since Christians were generally forbidden to make loans and charge interest, Jews were able to play an important role as bankers and moneylenders in many places.

Governments were often tolerant of Jews, especially when this proved profitable. But all too often during the Middle Ages, a ruler needing money would expel the Jews from the area under his control and take all of their property and belongings. This happened in Paris in 1182; sixteen years later the banished Jews were allowed to return to the city, but only after paying a tax to the king. Even worse, Jews were sometimes targets of extreme violence; in 1190, 150 Jewish men, women, and children were killed in a riot in the city of York, England. Europe's Christian majority still had a long way to go toward understanding and accepting religious differences.

A Jewish religious teacher in medieval Italy, with a prayer shawl draped over his head, reverently carries a scroll of the Torah, the first five books of the Bible.

RELIGION AND EVERYDAY LIFE

Many people have called the Middle Ages the Age of Faith. However, it can be difficult to know how ordinary women and men understood their religion. For one thing, church services were given almost entirely in Latin, the official language of the Church. Sometimes a priest would preach a sermon in the people's everyday language, explaining the Bible and the Church's teachings in ways that people could understand. Very few could read the Bible for themselves. It was written in Latin—and besides, the average medieval European could not read at all.

However, the Church was strongly supported by most rulers and nobles, and it played a major role in education and the arts. Christian ideas, values, and symbols were present in nearly every facet of society. And though there were differences between nations and between social classes, there seems to have been a general feeling among most western Europeans that they were united by Christianity.

Medieval Christians marked important stages of their lives by observing the sacraments of the Church. The sacraments were ceremonies that both demonstrated God's grace and bestowed it on those taking part. Soon after birth, a baby was welcomed into the Church by the sacrament of baptism. The sacrament of confirmation followed, either immediately or around the age of seven, to make the baptism complete. In the sacrament of confession, or penance, a person confessed his or her sins to God through a priest, and the priest assigned a penance for the person to perform to atone for the sins. (The penance often took the form of saying a

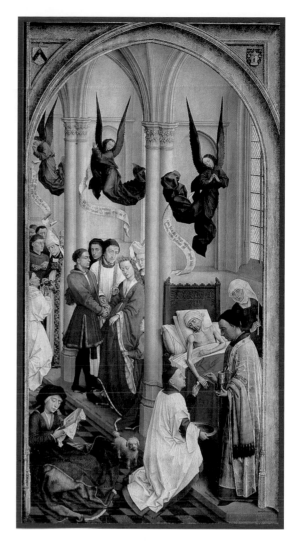

A priest anoints the hands of a dying man in the sacrament of extreme unction.

certain number of prayers.) The other sacrament that every medieval Christian expected to go through was extreme unction. Someone who was thought to be close to death would make a last confession to a priest. After forgiving the confessed sins, the priest anointed the person's body with holy oil in preparation for death.

Most people also took part in the sacrament of matrimony, or marriage. But priests, monks, and nuns were not allowed to marry. With the sacrament of holy orders, men dedicated their lives to the Church by joining the priesthood.

2
THE FAITH OF A CONTINENT

In the Middle Ages, as now, Christianity was based on belief in one all-powerful, all-knowing God, present everywhere all the time. This same belief was also held by Jews and Muslims. Christianity, however, taught that the one God was revealed as three "persons," distinct from one another yet completely unified. The three-in-one, or Trinity, was made up of God the Father, God the Son, and God the Holy Spirit. The Son was Jesus Christ, and his life and teachings were the centerpoint of Christianity.

Jesus was a Jew who lived in the kingdom of Judaea (now Israel) from around 4 BCE to 30 CE. The Bible tells that Jesus was born as a human in order to save people from their sins. His mother was Mary, the wife of a carpenter named Joseph. Before Jesus was born, the angel Gabriel visited Mary to tell her that she would become pregnant with a son who would be great and holy. When it was time for the birth, Mary and Joseph were away from home and had to take shelter in a stable. Angels appeared to shepherds nearby to tell them of the holy infant, and a bright star guided wise men from the East to the birthplace. Shepherds and wise men alike knelt in homage to the newborn baby.

Shown on a stained glass window at Canterbury Cathedral in England, a star leads the three wise men from the East to the birthplace of the baby Jesus.

When Jesus was around thirty years old, he went to his cousin John for baptism. This was a ceremony in which John symbolically cleansed people of their past sins so that they could begin to live more righteous lives. For the next three years Jesus traveled through Judaea, performing miracles, healing the sick, and teaching. Many of his lessons centered on the power of love—"You shall love your neighbor as yourself" (Matthew 22:39)—and the importance of the

Golden Rule—"Whatever you wish that men would do to you, do so to them" (Matthew 7:12). He also taught that those who believed in him and followed his teachings would have an eternal life in the presence of God. Jesus attracted a large number of followers, both women and men. Twelve of these followers, the disciples or apostles, were his most devoted students.

Judaea was part of the Roman Empire, and some people feared that Jesus was trying to start a rebellion and would make himself king of the Jews. He was arrested and put on trial. Condemned to death by the Romans, he was crucified, or executed by being hung on a cross. Three days later, the Bible says, some of his women followers went to his tomb and found it empty. An angel told them that Jesus had been resurrected—he had risen from the dead. After this Jesus appeared several times to his followers, promising forgiveness of sins and resurrection to all who believed in him. Then he ascended to heaven to rejoin God the Father.

SPEAKING UP FOR HUMANITY

Like many Christians today, Christians of the Middle Ages honored a large number of saints. The saints were people who had lived exceptionally holy lives and who had the power to perform miracles. Saints were believed to dwell in heaven. Although God was the only divine power in the universe, he was often felt to be unreachable. So if a Christian needed something, she or he might pray to a saint, believing that the saint would then "speak to" God on their behalf.

When seeking a saint's help, a person often prayed before a picture or statue of the saint or, if possible, at a shrine to the saint. Some shrines housed a saint's relics, objects associated with the saint or even some of the saint's physical remains (usually bones). Holy relics had a great reputation for miraculous powers.

People, countries, cities, churches, and organizations of crafts people usually had one or more patron saints. The patron saint was

One of the most important and beloved saints of medieval Europe was Francis of Assisi. In this painting by the great Italian artist Giotto, Francis kneels before the pope, who gives his blessing to the new religious society that Francis has started.

the special protector of the person or group, who would in turn be especially devoted to this saint. Often a patron saint was chosen because of some similarity between an event in the saint's life and the activities of a particular group. For example, a popular story was told of Saint Crispin, a young Roman nobleman who became a Christian. As he traveled from place to place to preach the new religion, he supported himself as a shoemaker. In one town, he made shoes for many poor people, refusing any payment for his work. At night angels came and gave him leather to make more shoes for the poor. Because of this, Saint Crispin was regarded as the patron saint of shoemakers and other leatherworkers.

The most important and best-loved of all the saints was Mary, the mother of Jesus. She had always been important to Christians, but devotion to her grew tremendously during the High Middle Ages. Great churches, cathedrals, and monasteries were dedicated to her, such as the cathedrals of Notre Dame in Paris and Chartres, France. (*Notre Dame* means "Our Lady," one of Mary's titles.) Songs were sung in her praise not only in church but also in noble courts. Tales of her life and of the miracles she worked for those who prayed to her were popular in books and with preachers and storytellers, too. To medieval Christians, Mary was the merciful Mother of God, the Queen of Heaven, and the most perfect human being who had ever lived.

3
CHRISTIAN COMMUNITIES

he medieval Church owed much of its strength to its organization. All of western Christendom was divided into parishes.

Parish basically means "neighborhood"; a parish could be two or three small villages, a single village, or a section of a large village or town. Every parish had its own priest and its own church and cemetery. A number of parishes were grouped together to form a diocese, which was overseen by a bishop. An archbishop had charge of a group of dioceses, called an archdiocese. Above the archbishops were the cardinals, who were counselors and assistants to the pope.

The pope was the bishop of Rome. According to tradition, the first bishop of Rome was Jesus' disciple Saint Peter, whose name means "rock." Before Jesus died, he had said to Peter, "On this rock I will build my church. . . . I will give you the keys of the kingdom of heaven" (Matthew 16:18–19). Because of these statements, the pope, regarded as Saint Peter's successor, was the head of the entire Church.

An abbot oversees workers who are constructing a new church and other buildings for the religious community he heads.

FROM VILLAGE CHURCH TO SOARING CATHEDRAL

Most medieval people's religious lives centered around their parish church. In many villages, the church was the only building constructed of stone. It was often a small, plain building, perhaps decorated with a few wall paintings showing scenes from the Bible. Until late in the Middle Ages, there were usually no pews—people had to stand, sit on the floor, or bring stools or benches from home. The parish church also functioned as a kind of community center, a place where meetings and other gatherings could be held.

Cathedrals were the churches where bishops had their headquarters. Located in important cities, they were built to be as large and awe-inspiring as possible. Some cathedrals took more than a hundred years to build. No effort or expense was spared to make them beautiful, to the glory of God and the Church.

From tiny village church to towering cathedral, most medieval Christian houses of worship were built according to a similar plan. They often took the approximate shape of a cross.

The most important part of the church was the choir, or chancel. This was always in the east of the building. Here was the high altar, where priests conducted Mass, the main religious service. The altar, made of stone, was on a raised platform reached by three steps, which symbolized the Trinity. At the back of the altar there might be an altarpiece—a painting or carved panel showing stories from the life of Jesus or the saints. In cathedrals and other large churches the altarpiece was usually an elaborate work of art. The choir was only for members of the clergy and

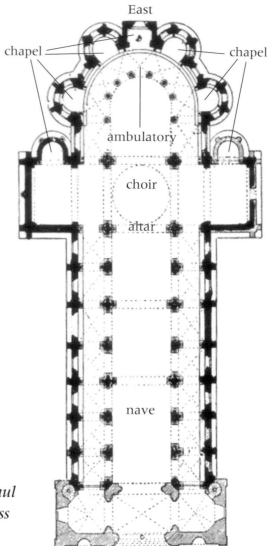

East

chapel

chapel

ambulatory

choir

altar

nave

This diagram of the Church of Saint Paul in Issoire, France, shows the typical cross shape of many medieval churches.

often was separated from the main part of the church by a screen carved out of wood or stone.

While the priests chanted the Mass and other services, the people listened from the nave. This was the central section of the church. On the north side of the nave there was a pulpit, a kind of platform raised up high. A priest stood here when he preached a sermon. Some churches also had pulpits built into their outside walls so that preachers could give sermons outdoors.

Behind the choir, large medieval churches often had a place called an ambulatory. Priests and other worshipers could walk up the aisles along the nave and around the ambulatory in religious processions.

Radiating off the ambulatory, there might be several chapels. Chapels could be located in other parts of a church, too. These chapels were semi-enclosed rooms, each with its own altar dedicated to a particular saint. A chapel devoted to the Virgin Mary was called a Lady chapel; a large number of medieval churches had one.

A PLACE APART

Parish priests and the churchmen at cathedrals served God and their fellow Christians in the everyday world. But many religious people in the Middle Ages wished to be able to leave the world behind and turn all their thoughts to God. There were numerous monasteries where they could do this, at least to some extent. A monastery was a place where a group of men or women lived as a community of monks or nuns, devoting themselves to prayer and study. (Today monasteries for women are usually called convents, or sometimes nunneries.) A few of these communities were double monasteries, for both men and women. The monks and nuns lived and worked in separate buildings from each other, but they shared a church and were governed by a single superior officer.

A monastery ruled by an abbot (the highest rank of monk) or abbess (the highest rank of nun) was called an abbey. It had to have at least twelve monks or nuns. A priory was a monastery headed by a prior or prioress, the second highest rank for monks or nuns. Priories could be smaller than abbeys and were under the

GLORY TO GOD IN STONE, GLASS, AND PAINT

Among the most outstanding remains of medieval times are abbeys, churches, and cathedrals. Many of these buildings are still places of worship today.

Two basic styles of building were used for medieval houses of worship. The earlier style is now called Romanesque. Like ancient Roman structures, Romanesque buildings featured many rounded arches. In the twelfth century a new style emerged, which is known as Gothic architecture. Gothic buildings had tall, pointed arches. Thanks to new engineering techniques, stone structures now soared to lofty heights, naturally drawing worshipers' eyes up toward heaven.

The new architecture also allowed large windows to be set into the high walls of the cathedrals and churches. Colored glass was easier to produce at this time than perfectly clear glass, so church designers made a virtue of necessity and created stained glass windows. The first stained glass windows were simple designs, but artists soon realized that they could make pictures with the glass. Stained glass windows illustrating stories from the Bible and other religious scenes became an important feature of churches from then on.

Cathedrals and other churches were also adorned with sculptures. The portals, or entryways, of cathedrals had particularly impressive sculptures. The tympanum, the arching space above the doorway, was a place where the most important religious scenes were carved. Cathedrals also had sculptures of saints, kings and queens, and imaginary creatures.

Other kinds of artwork could be found as well. Floors, walls, and even ceilings might be decorated with mosaics, tiny pieces of colored stone laid together to form designs or pictures. Choir stalls, where the clergy sat during services, often featured ornate wood carvings. The candlesticks and other objects on the altar could be masterpieces of metalwork.

Paintings decorated many churches. Some of medieval Europe's greatest artworks were painted altarpieces. The walls and ceilings of churches were often painted, too, sometimes very elaborately. For example, between 1290 and 1296, the artist Giotto produced a series of wall paintings about the life of Saint Francis to adorn a new church in Assisi. Such paintings helped bring biblical figures, saintly role models, and Christian teachings to life for all worshipers.

This view of the inside of Sainte-Chapelle in Paris shows the beauty and detail of Gothic arches and stained glass windows. Sainte-Chapelle was built by the French king Louis IX as his royal chapel, and it housed many important religious relics.

authority of abbeys. For example, there were more than three hundred priories dependent on the great abbey of Cluny, France.

Some monasteries were on the outskirts or even in the middle of cities—a prime example of this is Westminster Abbey in London. Other religious communities were in the countryside or in lonely places such as forests or islands. Very often, however, a village or town would grow up outside a monastery's or abbey's walls. When this happened, sometimes the religious community would uproot itself and move to another, more isolated place.

The center of a monastery was its cloister. A cloister is a square or rectangular covered walkway around a garden or open area. Many cloisters were enclosed, with glass windows looking out on the garden. Monks and nuns might spend hours each day in such a cloister, which often had alcoves where they could sit to read, pray, or meditate. The stone floors of these cloisters were strewn with sweet-smelling rushes, and in cold weather braziers could be set up for warmth.

From the cloister, monks and nuns could get to other important rooms and buildings, such as the monastery's church. There was also a chapter house, the business center of the monastery. The refectory was the building where monks and nuns had their meals. Just outside the refectory might be a lavatorium, a place for washing up. Nearby was the community's kitchen.

Monastery residents slept in a dormitory. This was either a large open room with a number of beds, or a room divided into

The abbey of Vallombrosa in northern Italy was dedicated to Saint Mary, the mother of Jesus. Vallombrosa was a large and thriving monastery, and the monks ran a school that was famous for centuries.

small cells, each containing little more than a bed. A "night stair" often led from the dormitory directly to the church so that the residents could easily get to nighttime services.

Large monasteries might have many other buildings besides those around the cloister. The superior (the monk or nun who was the head of the monastery) sometimes had a separate house. There could be workshops for different crafts, stables for horses, barns, a mill for grinding grain, and guest houses. Guests entered the monastery through a gatehouse. This was also a place where poor people came to receive food, clothing, and other assistance from the monks or nuns.

Large abbeys frequently owned farms, forests, flocks of sheep, fishing rights on rivers, ships, and other property outside the monastery walls. The great wealth of many abbeys not only supported their residents and aided the neighboring poor, but also allowed the creation of masterpieces of building, art, and writing.

4
MEN OF GOD

There were many ways for a medieval man to serve in the Church. Men who took holy orders, dedicating themselves to the religious life, were members of the clergy. The secular clergy were those who were out in the world, interacting with people on a day-to-day basis. They might be parish priests, bishops, or cathedral officials. The regular clergy were those who lived according to a set of guidelines called a rule (*regula* in Latin). The regular clergy, mainly monks, usually lived apart from the world. Monks could also be priests, and many were.

"IN THE WORLD BUT NOT OF IT"

There were several grades of secular clergy. The lowest ones were called the minor orders. Originally they each had specific duties, but by the High Middle Ages they were mainly stages in the education of a priest. Some men remained in minor orders all their lives, though. Their training enabled them to take up important positions in government and in noble households, among other things. A noble's treasurer, for example, was very often a cleric in minor orders. Other clerics in minor orders might teach in schools or universities.

Bernard of Clairvaux, who was declared a saint after his death, preaches to his fellow monks.

It generally took many years of study and devotion to become a priest. Once a man reached the major orders, the higher grades of clergy, he began to take on definite responsibilities in religious services. Finally, at the age of twenty-five, having moved through all the other orders, a man could become a priest. As a priest, he was empowered to offer Holy Communion (the most important part of Mass), to preach, to bless, and to forgive sins. He could administer all the sacraments except confirmation and holy orders. If he was a parish priest, his main duty was to use these powers to care for the souls of the people of his parish. Someday, through hard work and good fortune, he might become a bishop. Then he would be able to administer all the sacraments, and would have the supervision and care of all the priests in his diocese.

Although the secular clergy lived and worked among the people, they were set off from them in important ways. The visible sign of the clergy's dedication to religion was the tonsure, a special haircut that left the top of the head bald. Clergymen were not required to serve in the military or to pay taxes. They were forbidden to engage in buying and selling, loaning money, and similar trades. They were allowed, however, to work outside the Church to earn their living if necessary. They were also instructed to avoid gambling, hunting, and other unsuitable pastimes. People in holy orders, if accused of crimes, could only be tried by the Church's courts.

Clerics in the major orders were not supposed to marry. However, until the twelfth century it was fairly common for a country priest to have a wife and children. This seems to have been accepted by the local peasants, but Church authorities frowned on it. Eventually the Church established severe penalties for married clergymen and their wives and children. Church leaders feared that priests with wives and children would be distracted by family life from giving all of their time and energy to God's service.

LIVING BY THE RULE

Almost from the beginnings of Christianity, there had been people who wanted to withdraw from the world and turn all their attention to God. Many such people went out into wilderness areas and lived alone as hermits. Others gathered together in small communities devoted to the religious life; these were the first monasteries. Around the year 529, Saint Benedict founded a new monastery in Italy. Benedict wrote a book of rules to guide his monks. The Rule of Saint Benedict became the basis of monastery life for centuries to come.

All monks vowed themselves, for the rest of their lives, to poverty (they were not allowed to own any personal property), chastity (they could not marry or have relationships with women), and obedience (to the head of the monastery and to the Church's teachings). The Rule gave further guidance to their lives. It covered everything from what sort of man should be chosen abbot and how religious services should be conducted to how much the monks should eat and what their clothing should be made of. All of this was designed to help the monks think of God and the monastery community before themselves. Everything was owned in common, by the monastery as a whole. Clothing, food, and tools were distributed to each monk according to his need.

The abbot was the supreme authority in any monastery. His deputy was the prior. In an abbey the prior assisted the abbot, while in a priory he supervised the monks on the abbot's behalf. In both abbey and priory, one monk was appointed as cellarer. His job was to oversee the monks' food supplies; if the monastery was a large one, he was allowed to have several assistants. The porter was an elderly monk who lived in a cell near the monastery door. It was his responsibility to admit guests and to distribute food and clothing to the needy when they came to the monastery. Another important position in many monasteries was that of infirmarian. This monk was in charge of taking care of the sick, usually with the help of medicinal herbs grown in the monastery garden. Some monasteries gave treatment not only to their residents but also to local poor people. There were other offices as well, especially in large monasteries; but no matter what office a monk held, he was always to be humble about it.

In spite of the Rule's emphasis on humility, simplicity, and separation from the world, many abbeys became so large, wealthy, and powerful that some monks decided they needed to make reforms. In 1098 Saint Robert of Molêsme founded a new abbey at Cîteaux (see-TOH), France, and demanded that his monks return to strictly following the Rule. This began a movement that spread throughout Europe in the twelfth century and resulted in the creation of a new religious society, the Cistercian Order. Several other orders were created and flourished during this time, too, but the Cistercian Order was the largest and most influential.

The Cistercians gave a prominent role to lay brothers. These were men who took the same vows as the monks but did not participate in the daily religious services, which monks were required to do. Instead, the lay brothers were responsible for cooking; cleaning; grinding grain; making repairs; constructing buildings; and making such things as candles, parchment (animal skin specially prepared for writing on), and blankets and clothing. The lay brothers also did a great deal of farmwork, raising crops and livestock both to supply the monks and to sell for the support of the monastery. This work allowed Cistercian monasteries to be entirely self-sufficient and cut off from the world.

Lay brothers usually lived in their own building at the monastery. But many Cistercian abbeys owned widely scattered farms, called granges. The lay brothers who did the farmwork lived at the granges. Each farm was in the charge of a lay brother with the title "master of the grange." No matter how far the grange was from its abbey, the master of the grange and the other lay brothers were usually expected to return to the abbey for Sunday services every week and for services on important holidays.

IN THE FOOTSTEPS OF THE DISCIPLES

In the first part of the thirteenth century, a new wave of religious feeling produced new kinds of religious societies. These were called the mendicant orders, from the Latin word that means "begging," because their members embraced total poverty and were supported completely by charity. The main mendicant orders were the Franciscans, founded by Saint Francis of Assisi, and the Dominicans, founded by Saint Dominic. Members of these orders were called friars, meaning "brothers."

Saint Francis was the son of a wealthy Italian cloth merchant. As a young man, Francis was a soldier and lived a life of pleasure, caring more for fine clothes than for God. Still, he was always generous to the poor. Then, during the course of a battle, he was captured, and for a year he remained a prisoner of war. The experience changed him. More and more his thoughts turned to religion. After a time, his holiness and charity began to attract followers.

In church one day, Francis heard the Gospel reading in which Jesus instructs his disciples to go out into the world: "And preach as you go, saying, 'The kingdom of heaven is at hand.' Heal the sick, raise the dead, cleanse lepers, cast out demons. You received without pay, give without pay. Take no gold, nor silver, nor copper in your belts, no bag for your journey, nor two tunics, nor sandals, nor a staff. . . ." (Matthew 10: 7–10). This was exactly what Francis wanted to do, and he was inspired to write a rule for himself and his followers. They gave away everything they owned and traveled

THE SONG OF BROTHER SUN

In the twentieth century, Saint Francis of Assisi became very well known for his close relationship to nature. In 1979 the pope even named him the patron saint of ecology. In "The Song of Brother Sun," Saint Francis expresses his joy in the natural world and God's part in it. Francis was always singing and dancing in praise of God. (In fact, he sometimes called himself and his followers the Minstrels of God.) In many churches today, people still sing a hymn based on the saint's words. Here is a modern English version of Francis's song:

Praise be to you, my Lord, with all your creatures,
especially Sir Brother Sun,
who is the day and through whom you give us light.
And he is beautiful and radiant with great splendor
and bears a likeness of you, Most High One.
Praise be to you, my Lord, through Sister Moon and the stars;
in heaven you formed them clear and precious and beautiful.
Praise be to you, my Lord, through Brother Wind,
and through the air, cloudy and serene, and every kind of weather.
Praise be to you, my Lord, through Sister Water—
so useful and humble and precious and pure.
Praise be to you, my Lord, through Brother Fire,
through whom you light the night,
and he is beautiful and playful and robust and strong.
Praise be to you, my Lord, through our Sister Mother Earth,
who sustains and governs us,
and who produces many kinds of fruit and colored flowers and herbs.
Praise be to you, my Lord, through our Sister Death,
from whom no one living can escape.
Praise and bless my Lord and give him thanks,
*   and serve him with great humility.*

Saint Francis's legend tells of him speaking with, preaching to, and caring for animals on many occasions. In this painting by Giotto, Francis preaches to a flock of birds.

from place to place, taking with them nothing but the simple, rough woolen robes on their backs. Everywhere they went, they preached and helped the poor. Eventually the Franciscans had many monasteries, where they lived very simply—but never permanently, for it was always their mission to be out among the people, following in the steps of Jesus' disciples.

Saint Dominic was inspired by this example. The order he founded also had a mission to send preachers out among the people. The Dominicans' special concerns were to improve people's morals and to make certain their beliefs were in line with official Church teachings. Dominicans were often highly educated, with a thorough knowledge of the Church's history and laws, so that they could be effective preachers.

THE CANONS

A middle way between the secular and regular clergy was occupied by men known as canons. They lived by a rule that medieval people believed was set down by Saint Augustine in the fifth century. At the same time, they were "in the world," for they, too, were trying to follow in the footsteps of the disciples, in particular by doing good works among the people. Many groups of canons ran hospitals, for example, to help the poor. Canons could also serve as parish priests.

Most canons lived in houses together. These houses were usually in cities, but occasionally they could be in very isolated places. Some canons, known as secular canons, did not give up personal property but lived in homes of their own. These canons were generally associated with managing the affairs of cathedrals and often ran schools.

WARRIOR MONKS

The Church taught that all people were basically sinful but that acts of penance could earn forgiveness for sin. One of the most powerful acts of penance was going on a pilgrimage, a journey to an important religious site. The greatest pilgrimage was to Jerusalem, the scene of Jesus' death and resurrection. In 1095 the pope sent out a call for knights to go to Jerusalem to take the city from its Muslim rulers. This was the beginning of the First Crusade, a pilgrimage and at the same time a war fought for God.

The crusaders won Jerusalem and other parts of the holy land, where they established their own kingdoms. Many Europeans settled there. Some of them formed groups dedicated to protecting and caring for the pilgrims who came in growing numbers now that Jerusalem was in Christian hands. These groups eventually became religious orders of knights. By 1200 there were two major orders, the Knights Templar and the Knights Hospitaller.

In both, full members took the lifetime monastic vows of poverty, chastity, and obedience. They lived in communities and followed a rule. The Templars' rule was based on that of Saint Benedict, while the Hospitallers followed the Rule of Saint Augustine. There were four kinds of members: brothers knight, brothers sergeant (less heavily armed, lower-ranking warriors), brothers at service (who were not fighters), and chaplains (the orders' priests). When knights and sergeants were not out fighting the Muslims, they were expected to participate in the full round of daily religious services or to say a set number of prayers every day. Most of the rest of their time was probably spent in military training.

A crusader kneels in prayer. Behind him, his horse also appears to kneel.

In the Middle East, Templars and Hospitallers lived in castles that were a combination of fortress and monastery. The military orders eventually had many members in Europe, too. Here they lived in smaller communities, known as commanderies. In some cities, such as London, the Templars and Hospitallers had large, grand churches, which for many people symbolized the holy city of Jerusalem itself.

5
BRIDES OF CHRIST

In the early years of Christianity, women played an active role in spreading and supporting the new religion. Throughout the Middle Ages, the Church continued to give women roles in religion. Women could not join the secular clergy, but they could join monasteries and become nuns. As nuns, they made the same lifelong vows of poverty, chastity, and obedience that monks did. A nun's vows were sealed by a ring that she wore to show that she had turned away from marriage and the world and was wedded to Christ. As a bride of Christ, she or her family also paid a dowry to the monastery. The dowry—a payment

in the form of money or property—could be quite large, although not as large as if she were actually getting married.

Nuns faced many of the same prejudices and restrictions as other medieval women. The Church taught that women were naturally more sinful than men, and that women distracted men from religion. Women were generally not allowed into men's monasteries, and they were not allowed to come near any church altar during Mass. The Church forbade women to preach, to serve as priests, or even to assist priests during religious services.

Outside the Church there were also many negative opinions and laws about women. Although peasant women worked in the fields alongside men, and city women worked at almost every trade that men did, women were still thought of as weaker and less intelligent than men. Most authorities believed that women had to have the protection and guidance of men, and many laws reflected this.

Nearly all women's monasteries were supervised by men, usually the abbot of a men's monastery of the same order, or the bishop of the local diocese. Women's monasteries also had to

This fifteenth-century tapestry shows a young woman's path to the religious life. At first she is troubled, but she goes to a priest and, kneeling prayerfully, confesses her sins. After purifying her heart, she receives Holy Communion. Then, at last, she goes to a monastery to become a nun.

include male workers. Usually there was a male steward who represented the nuns in business matters. There would probably be some male servants to do the heaviest physical work and to guard the monastery. Most importantly, every house of nuns had at least one male chaplain. This priest (or sometimes a group of priests) conducted Mass for the nuns, heard their confessions, blessed them, and received the vows of new nuns. No woman was permitted to do any of these things.

However, there were some abbesses who defied the rules and did hear confessions, give blessings, and preach in public. In fact, the abbess of a large and wealthy monastery—like the abbot of such a place—could become a very powerful, influential person. If her abbey owned a great deal of land, she would be the lord of all the people who lived and worked on it. She would judge their cases in court, punish criminals, impose fines and fees, control land use, set up fairs and markets, and exercise other rights and powers. Sometimes an abbess might have a great deal of authority in her diocese as well. She might even have the right to approve the appointments of the diocese's priests. All this was in addition to supervising the nuns and chaplains of her monasteries. In a double monastery, such as the Abbey of Fontevrault (fohn-teh-VROH) in France, even the monks might be under the rule of an abbess.

A CLOISTERED LIFE

Most women's monasteries followed the Rule of Saint Benedict and were run almost exactly like the men's Benedictine monasteries. The monastery's offices were the same, only filled by women:

abbess, prioress, cellaress, and so on. However, in Cistercian communities, lay sisters did not have quite the same role as lay brothers. Instead of spending time living and working at monastic granges, lay sisters remained in the monastery. There, like lay brothers, they did much of the monastery's physical and practical work so that nuns could be free for religious services, prayer, and study.

In the mendicant orders, the roles of women were very different from those of male members. Both Saint Francis and Saint Dominic personally founded monasteries for women. But both agreed—as did Church authorities—that women should not follow in the footsteps of the apostles as wandering preachers. Like other nuns, female members of the Franciscan and Dominican orders were not supposed to leave their monasteries, so they could not work among the poor as their brother monks did. However, they did give food and clothing to any poor people who came to the monastery gatehouse for help. And like nuns of other orders, sometimes they could affect the outside world by running schools for children (though usually only children of the upper classes).

A DIFFERENT CALLING

Many women thrived in the seclusion and discipline of a monastery. They appreciated the opportunity to devote themselves to prayer and study and the freedom from marriage and childbearing. Other women sought a more active religious life, not so completely separated from the world. Some also wished to serve God but not to take the lifetime vows of nuns.

Canonesses were women who lived in a religious community run according to the Rule of Saint Augustine. They did not give

ABBESS HILDEGARD

In 1105 a seven-year-old German girl was taken to a small monastery to receive a religious education. The girl, Hildegard, learned scripture, music, and Latin. At the age of fourteen she took vows and became a nun. Over the years she gained the respect of her fellow nuns, and at the age of thirty-eight they elected her as their abbess.

Hildegard had had religious visions since childhood. When she was forty-two, she had a vision in which the heavens opened up and flooded her brain with a brilliant light. The light warmed her all through, and she instantly understood the deepest meanings of scripture. As the experience ended, God commanded her to write down all of her visions from then on. At first Hildegard was reluctant because she doubted herself. But after a long illness, she began to record her religious experiences, often dictating them to her secretary, a monk named Volmar.

In Hildegard's time, many people sought to have mystical experiences like she did. They wanted to experience God in a direct and personal way and to see visions that revealed his purposes and his glory. Church authorities were often suspicious of mystics, though, because sometimes their visions were not in line with official teachings. Hildegard was very anxious about this. She wrote to the great and influential Cistercian monk Bernard of Clairvaux (clair-VOH) to ask for his blessing. Bernard in turn showed some chapters of Hildegard's first book to the pope. The pope wrote to her, full of admiration and praise. From this point on, Hildegard never doubted herself.

Hildegard's monastery was growing, and around the year 1150 she moved it to Rupertsberg, near Bingen, Germany. Eventually she had fifty nuns and two chaplains under her rule. Even more people came under her influence. She became famous not only in Germany but also in France, Flanders (now Belgium), England, Italy, and even Greece. Large numbers of people wrote to her for her advice. Over the rest of her life, she corresponded with various abbesses, bishops, university professors, and nobles, and also with several queens and kings, two emperors, four popes, and at least two future saints (Bernard of Clairvaux and Thomas à Becket).

Along with her visionary works, Hildegard wrote books that dealt with science, philosophy, medicine, and natural history. She was also gifted musically. She was one of medieval Europe's greatest composers of religious chants, writing hymns and other religious music. She composed some musical plays, too, which the nuns of her monastery probably performed. Hildegard described music as a way of recapturing the original beauty and joy of paradise.

Hildegard of Bingen was eighty-one when she died in 1179. In her last years, she wrote of the light that she always saw in her spirit and the living light that was the love of God. During her long life she was able to shine that light upon many others, and to make the most of opportunities that few other medieval women enjoyed.

up personal property, and they could return to "the world" whenever they wished. They vowed chastity and obedience for the time they lived in the community, but they did not have to keep these vows after they left. Canonesses might also live in their own homes, continuing to follow the Augustinian Rule.

The Franciscans and Dominicans both recognized that there were many women who wished to dedicate themselves to religion but could not join monasteries because they were already married (or sometimes for other reasons). These women could become tertiaries, members of what was sometimes called the Franciscan or Dominican Third Order. Tertiaries lived in their own homes. Married men could also become tertiaries, under the same conditions, and it sometimes happened that both members of a couple would decide to take the vows of tertiaries. They still lived together, but as brother and sister instead of as husband and wife.

Canonesses and women tertiaries frequently dedicated themselves to caring for the sick. They might work alongside monks in hospitals such as Paris's famous Hôtel de Dieu ("hostel of God"). During the Middle Ages, hospitals cared for the poor, and often for orphans and widows, as well as the sick. By doing these good works, many canonesses and tertiaries felt they were following in the footsteps of the disciples in ways that nuns in monasteries never could.

THE INDEPENDENT BEGUINES

There was another kind of religious life for women, created by women themselves. Beginning in the late twelfth century in what is now Belgium, groups of women known as Beguines chose to

Nuns or canonesses at the Hôtel de Dieu in Paris teaching girls how to care for sick people.

dedicate themselves to religion in a new way. They did not enter monasteries or make lifetime vows. They lived simply but did not embrace poverty. They could get married if they wanted to.

The Beguine movement spread from Belgium to Germany and France. There were many differences among the various groups of Beguines, but they all had a common desire to live the way Jesus and his disciples had lived: not only spending lots of time in prayer but also working among the poor and sick. Some Beguines were so enthusiastic about the religious life that they preached sermons and debated religious issues publicly—activities forbidden to women by the Church. There were other Beguines who defied Church law and translated the Bible from Latin into German and French so that ordinary people could read it.

The first Beguines were mostly from noble or rich merchant families. But the movement soon attracted numerous working and poor women. Many women in these lower classes desired a religious life, but most could not afford to join monasteries, and many did not want to be so totally cut off from the rest of human

The Beguine movement in Belgium lasted for many centuries. The Beguinage of Bruges, founded in 1245, still housed Beguines in the nineteenth century, when artist Archibald Kay painted this scene.

society. Beguines spent much of their day in prayer and helping the poor, but they also usually worked for their living. Spinning, weaving, sewing, doing laundry, and caring for the sick were the most common trades worked by Beguines. In addition, some Beguines ran schools in various medieval cities.

At first Beguines lived in their own or their parents' homes. Gradually, groups of Beguines began to live together in houses, dividing their days between work, prayer, and charity. The late thirteenth century saw the creation of large beguinages, which were almost miniature cities. The Great Beguinage in the Belgian city of Ghent, for example, had more than a hundred houses, two churches, a hospital, and a brewery.

Soon after this, however, the Church began to break up beguinages. While many churchmen admired the Beguines, others were suspicious of them because of their independence.

6

GROWING UP IN THE CHURCH

Some people, particularly lay brothers and sisters, entered religious service as adults. If a woman's husband died, she might go to live in a monastery instead of remarrying or staying on her own. There were also men who joined monasteries when their wives died. Many of these widows and widowers had always been deeply religious, like Saint Birgitta (or Bridget) of Sweden, who founded a double monastery after her husband's death. Others, like Eleanor of Aquitaine, the queen of England, retired to monasteries in order to live quieter, protected lives, but did not make any religious vows.

Most priests, monks, and nuns, however, began their life in the Church when they were children. Although many had humble origins, most were children of nobles and wealthy city dwellers. Usually their parents had made the decision to dedicate them to religion. This happened frequently in the case of younger sons, who by law would not inherit the family property. Younger daughters, too, were often marked for the religious life, since many families could provide dowries for only one or two daughters. Occasionally parents would promise God that they

Parents bring their son to a monastery to be educated, and probably to become a monk when he is old enough.

would dedicate a child to the religious life even before the baby was born, but generally the decision was made several years later.

It was also common for nobles to send physically or mentally handicapped children to monasteries. This may sound heartless—and numerous churchmen objected to the practice—but in medieval Europe, many of these children would not have been able to support themselves as adults. In a monastery, they would be cared for their entire lives. Orphaned children, too, were commonly dedicated to religious service. Usually the orphan's guardians believed this was the best way to give the child a secure future. Occasionally, however, the guardians simply wanted to help themselves to the child's inheritance.

Sometimes older children or teenagers felt a strong calling to go into the religious life even if their parents did not wish them to. For noble sons who did not want to be knights and for wealthy merchants' sons who did not want to go into business, entering the Church was also a sensible way to make their living. For upper-class girls who did not want to marry, becoming a nun was the only respectable alternative to becoming a wife and mother. It was also very often their only opportunity to pursue an education and use their talents. But whether young people joined the Church because of the desire for freedom and opportunity, for practical reasons, or because of devotion to God—or for all these reasons—they sometimes had great difficulty with their families because of their decision. Nevertheless, it was the nuns and churchmen who chose the religious life for themselves who were generally happiest and most successful in the Church.

MONASTERY CHILDREN

Boys who entered monasteries had a difficult period of adjustment and training. They were constantly supervised by a senior monk, their teacher. They were never left by themselves or in groups of only children. They could not signal or speak to one another without the teacher's permission. In many places they were allowed to play for only one hour once a week or once a month. In some monasteries they were not allowed to play at all.

Girls being raised and educated in monasteries seem to have been allowed a little more playtime. (One reason for this may be that girls usually entered monasteries when they were five or six years old, much younger than most boys did.) Otherwise they had the same restrictions as boys. They did not always receive the same education, though. They did learn to read and write, and of course they were thoroughly instructed in religion. But few girls had the opportunity to master Latin or to study such things as science and law. On the other hand, many received training as scribes and artists, and there were women's monasteries that were well known for the books they produced.

Children in monasteries were expected to be respectful and disciplined. They attended all of the daily religious services, just as the adult monks and nuns did. But sometimes children were allowed to lie down on their seats, while the adults had to remain sitting upright.

According to Church law, young people who were educated in monasteries were free to decide not to become monks or nuns and could choose to leave the community after turning twelve years old. However, this rarely happened. Most monastery-raised children made their vows of poverty, chastity, and obedience between the ages of thirteen and sixteen and spent the rest of their lives in religious service.

LEARNING OUTSIDE THE CLOISTER

For boys who would become priests, religious education typically started around age seven. At this point a boy might receive his first tonsure, marking his entrance into holy orders. Now he would go to school to begin his training. He might attend a monastery school or a school run by the local parish church or cathedral.

The school day was ten or twelve hours long, from just after sunup to just before sundown. The children sat on hard benches listening to the teacher, reading, and reciting their lessons. There were only two breaks in the long day: an hour in the morning and an hour at lunchtime. Discipline was strict, and it was acceptable for teachers to whip students for misbehavior.

In elementary school, students learned to read both Latin and their everyday language. They were also taught some arithmetic and writing, along with prayers, hymns, and basic Christian beliefs. In some places, girls were able to attend elementary school alongside boys.

At the age of ten or twelve, boys could go on to grammar school. Here they received intense training in Latin so that they would be able to write and speak it fluently. They also learned the art of public speaking, a little science and law, and some music. They studied important books of philosophy, religion, and ancient literature. By the end of grammar school, they were supposed to have a thorough knowledge of the Bible and the Church's teachings.

Some boys concentrated on the art of handwriting. After mastering the difficult skill of writing on parchment with a quill pen, they would become scribes. In the era before the printing press was invented, all books were completely handmade, and scribes were very important. They made new copies of old books and wrote out new books that authors dictated to them.

Scribes at work in the scriptorium, or writing room, of a monastery.

Between the ages of fourteen and sixteen, a boy could begin attending a university. Here he would pursue in-depth study of literature, philosophy, religious thinking, and sometimes law. University education was not required for all priests, but most bishops had this higher education.

Monks could also follow this educational plan. Many boys went to elementary and sometimes grammar school before entering a monastery. Even after becoming monks, they might attend a university to complete their education. As an alternative to universities, the Franciscans and especially the Dominicans had their own centers of learning for their members.

7
THE WORK OF GOD

edieval thinkers divided society into three "estates": those who worked, those who fought and ruled, and those who prayed. The clergy, of course, belonged to the third estate, and prayer was the center of their lives, especially for those in monasteries. Some prayer was private, but most of it took place during regular church services.

In all churches, there were services throughout the day, every day. The main service was Mass. Its most important part was Holy Communion. This sacrament was modeled on the Last Supper, Jesus' final meal with his disciples. He had given them bread and wine, telling them that these were his body and blood, and bid them eat and drink in memory of him. At Communion the priest gave specially blessed wafers, called the Host, to the congregation, saying, *"Hoc est corpus Christi"* ("This is the body of Christ"). Wine was also blessed in the name of Jesus, but only the priests drank it. The Church taught that during Communion, Christ was truly present in the Host and the blessed wine.

Mass was celebrated every day, although weekday services were shorter and simpler than those on Sunday. In addition to Communion, hymns, prayers, and readings from the Bible were always part of Mass. Much of the service was sung or chanted, and

A priest celebrating Mass prays before an altar, watched over by Moses and Saint Paul.

nuns and churchmen often found great satisfaction in composing beautiful music for this most important religious celebration.

In addition to Mass, there were eight other services, known as the Divine Offices. These were ceremonies of prayer and praise. The offices included hymns, Bible verses, prayers, and from three to nine psalms (poems from the Book of Psalms in the Bible). In

Nuns sitting in their choir stalls sing one of the Divine Offices.

medieval monasteries and cathedrals, every word of these services was sung.

The first office was matins, which was sung a little after midnight or around 2:00 A.M. Lauds was held at dawn or even earlier. Prime, terce, sext, and none were roughly three hours apart, from about 6:00 A.M. to about 3:00 P.M. In the evening, vespers was celebrated. The final office before bed was compline. The Franciscans made this a special, longer service and encouraged ordinary people to attend it at the end of their workday. Church bells rang to signal the beginning of each service, marking the passage of time not only for nuns and churchmen, but also for everyone in the neighborhood of the church.

LIFE IN THE MONASTERY

Monastery life was built around the routine of Mass and the Divine Offices. The entire community attended Mass twice each day. After the morning service, monks or nuns wound their way through the cloister to their chapter house. Here they listened to a chapter of the rule being read aloud (this activity gave the building its name) and discussed monastery business and spiritual matters. Sometimes the abbot or a senior monk gave a lecture. This was also a time for everyone to examine their own conduct and one another's. If anyone's behavior was found faulty, the abbot or prior would discipline them.

After sext, around noon, the monks or nuns went to the lavatorium to wash their hands, which was often done with great ceremony. Then they went into the refectory for their first meal of the day. In summertime they were allowed to take a nap or read to themselves after this meal. They would have another meal in the evening, before vespers. In winter, however, they were supposed to have only one meal a day, in the middle of the afternoon. At every meal, one of the monks or nuns read aloud from a religious book. Everyone else listened and ate in total silence. If they needed to communicate, they had to use sign language. For example, if a monk made a circle with the thumbs and forefingers of both hands, it meant, "Please pass the bread."

The Rule of Saint Benedict instructed, "Idleness is the enemy of the soul; and therefore the brethren ought to be employed in manual labor at certain times, at others, in devout reading." Ideally, monks and nuns spent time every morning working and time every afternoon reading. The work could take many forms, including the cleaning and upkeep of the monastery, tending the community's beehives or gardens, making candlesticks or clothes, and copying out or illustrating books. When it was time for study, monks and nuns chose their reading from works of philosophy, religious thought, history, and ancient literature. On Sundays they were not supposed to work, unless they had assigned tasks such as serving the meals, but to spend all their free hours reading.

As time went on, monks and nuns did less actual work, unless they belonged to a very small or poor monastery. (Partly this was because large, wealthy monasteries could have many servants to do the physical labor.) Church services were getting longer and more elaborate. In many places, services took up almost every moment of the monks' or nuns' day, so that there was only time left for eating and sleeping. However, worship and prayer were felt to be the true work of the monasteries. The work of lay brothers and sisters allowed monks and nuns the freedom to follow this calling.

8
HOLY DAYS

Just as each day had its pattern, the year had its rhythm, too. The monastic routine varied according to the seasons. In the summer, monks and nuns took advantage of the longer hours of daylight to do more reading and study. Because of the lengthy day they were allowed two meals; because of the heat, they did less work. In winter, with its shorter days, monastery residents ate only one meal. They read less and did more work than in the summer—but they also got more sleep during the long hours of darkness. The passing of the year was also marked by many holy days. In fact, nearly every day of the calendar was dedicated to a saint or to the memory of an event in the life of Jesus or Mary. Parts of Mass and of the Divine Offices changed day by day to mark these milestones of the year.

Throughout Christendom, the greatest holy days were Christmas and Easter. (These, by the way, might be the only times all year that nuns and monks took baths.) Christmas marked the birth of Jesus. Before Christmas there was a time of preparation called Advent. When Christmas finally arrived, it was celebrated with three Masses, the first one being held at midnight. In the medieval Church, Christmas Day was a joyous but solemn holiday.

Many medieval holidays were celebrated with religious processions. Here a group of monks carry relics of Saint Nicholas, housed in a splendid container, while ordinary worshipers follow behind.

During the Christmas season, however, some not-so-serious customs were observed in many churches and monasteries. For example, on the Feast of Saint Nicholas (December 6), a "boy bishop" was chosen from among the children of the monastery school, grammar school, or cathedral choir. This boy was dressed up in elaborate robes and led a procession around the parish, giving his blessing to the people. Similarly, in some women's monasteries a young girl acted as abbess for a limited time.

The boy bishop, sitting on the bishop's throne in the cathedral, might also be part of the Feast of Fools, celebrated on or around January 1. During the Divine Offices on this day, clergy members sometimes wore masks or dressed up as women or had their clothes on inside out. They held their service books upside down and sang out-of-tune nonsense syllables. Instead of making their way around the church with dignity, they ran and leaped about. During Mass they munched on sausages and heehawed like donkeys at the end of the service—and the congregation heehawed in response. Church authorities strongly disapproved of these customs, but they were popular throughout Europe, especially France.

Very soon it was time to get serious again. The Christmas season ended on January 6 with the Feast of Epiphany. On this day church services recalled three important events in the life of Jesus: the wise men kneeling to honor him, his baptism, and his first miracle.

In February or March, Lent began. Lent, the forty days before Easter, was a time when people were expected to be mindful of their sins and to try to put themselves right with God. Monks and nuns were supposed to have only one meal a day during Lent. The Rule of Saint Benedict taught, "The life of a monk ought always to be a Lenten observance. . . . We advise that during these days of Lent he guard his life with all purity and at the same time wash away . . . all the shortcomings of other times. . . . Let us devote ourselves to tearful prayers, to reading and compunction of heart. . . . During these days, therefore, let us add something to the usual amount of our service . . . ; let [each one] withdraw from his body somewhat of food, drink, sleep, speech, merriment, and with the gladness of spiritual desire await holy Easter."

Toward the end of Lent came Palm Sunday, the beginning of Holy Week. Palm Sunday celebrated the arrival of Jesus in Jerusalem, when people strewed his way with palm branches. In the Middle Ages, priests blessed palm, olive, or willow branches. They then distributed the branches among worshipers, who carried them in a procession before Mass, singing joyful hymns. A large carved wooden figure of Jesus riding a donkey was often pulled along in this procession.

The Thursday of Holy Week recalled Jesus' Last Supper. Before the meal, Jesus had washed the feet of all his disciples. In the Middle Ages, poor people, the elderly, and children were invited to monasteries to have their feet washed and receive gifts of food and money. At Westminster Abbey in London, the abbot himself washed the feet of thirteen elderly men, while the monks washed the feet of children.

The next day, Good Friday, was a solemn day of mourning, for it commemorated the death of Jesus. On Saturday night monks, nuns, and secular clergymen decorated their churches. All of the bright, beautiful candlesticks, crosses, and other ornaments of the church had been covered or put away for Lent. Now they were brought out again, ready for the dawning of Easter morning. With as many as five hundred candles lighting the church, the celebration of the most holy day of the year began: At Easter Christians remembered the resurrection of Jesus and his promise of eternal life.

9

TROUBLE IN PARADISE

Nuns and churchmen of the Middle Ages were expected to live according to very high standards. They did not always succeed, for they were prone to the same human failings as everyone else. Nevertheless, they were often criticized for not living up to the Church's ideals. They were charged with being greedy, lazy, selfish, corrupt, stupid, and worse.

Sometimes the criticism was deserved. There were many country priests who did not understand the Latin words they said during Mass. There were many bishops who never visited their dioceses and who were more involved in politics than in religion. There were nuns who entertained guests in luxurious rooms at their monasteries and monks who ate till they were fat and drank till they were drunk. There were popes who sided with one European government against another and used their powers for their own personal ends. These situations were worse at some times than at others. Usually the periods of great corruption were followed by periods of great reform.

Throughout the High Middle Ages in western Europe, there seems to have been a large number of people sincerely seeking a

CHAUCER'S CHURCH PEOPLE

Geoffrey Chaucer, who lived from about 1340 to 1400, was one of the greatest writers in English literature. His most famous book is *The Canterbury Tales*, in which a group of people on a pilgrimage to the shrine of Saint Thomas à Becket in Canterbury entertain one another by telling stories. Among the pilgrims are a prioress, a monk, and a friar. None of them appear to be living entirely according to the ideals of religious orders. At the time Chaucer was writing, many people were very critical of monastic life and felt that most monks and nuns were too worldly. Chaucer seems to have agreed. Here, in a modern English adaptation, are his portraits of the prioress, the monk, and the friar.

THE PRIORESS

There was also a nun, a prioress,
Whose smiles were all simple and modest. . . .
And she was called Madame Eglentine.
Full well she sang the service divine. . . .
And certainly she was very likable,
And pleasant, in conduct most amiable.
She always took great pains to copy
Courtly ways; her manner was stately.
She wished to be held worthy of reverence.
Now, to tell about her conscience:
She was so charitable and so piteous
That she would weep if she saw a mouse
Caught in a trap, if it were bleeding or dead.
She had some lapdogs that she fed

The Prioress, a very refined and worldly nun

With roasted meat, or milk and the best bread. . . .
Her veil was pleated most delicately.
Her nose was graceful, her eyes glassy gray,
Her mouth full small, and soft and red,
And certainly she had a fair forehead. . . .
Her cloak was very neat, as I could see.
Wrapped around her arm was a rosary
Of small coral beads, with larger beads of green;
On it hung a brooch with a golden sheen
On which there was written a crowned A,
And then, in Latin, "Love conquers all."

THE MONK

A monk there was, all others surpassing—
An outrider who loved to go hunting,
A manly man, and very capable.
He had many a fine horse in the stable,
And when he rode, everyone might hear
His bridle jingling in a whistling wind as clear
And also as loud as the chapel bell.
In the monastery where this lord had his cell,
The rule of Saint Maure or of Saint Benedict
Was thought to be old and somewhat strict—
This same monk left old things in the past,
And followed the new trends till the last.
He did not give the worth of a plucked hen
For the text that says hunters are not holy men. . . .
Therefore he was a hard rider, all right.
He had greyhounds as swift as birds in flight.
Tracking and hunting for the hare
Was his passion; he would not stop for any care.

I saw his sleeves finely edged, near the hand,
With fur, and it was the finest in the land;
And to fasten his hood under his chin,
He had a golden, very curious pin—
At the larger end a love knot had pride of place.
His head was bald and shone like any glass,
And so did his face, as if with oil or sweat.
This lord was in good shape and very fat. . . .
He was no pale, pining, wasted ghost;
He loved a fat swan best of any roast.

THE FRIAR

There was a friar, who was merry and wild. . . .
He was friendly and very well loved
By wealthy landowners all around
And by worthy women of the town. . . .
He very nicely heard confession;
And so that he would get a good donation,
He went easy when he gave penance;
His absolution was not unpleasant. . . .
For many a man is so hard of heart,
That he will not weep although he is hurt;
Therefore, instead of weeping and saying prayers,
Men often give silver to the poor friars.
This friar's hood was always filled with knives
And pins and other gifts for fair housewives.
And certainly he had a merry voice
As he sang and played his instrument of choice. . . .
He was as strong as a champion.

Geoffrey Chaucer. In The Canterbury Tales, *he described himself as one of the pilgrims to the shrine of Saint Thomas à Becket.*

He knew the taverns well in every town,
And knew every barmaid and innkeeper
Better than he knew any beggar or leper.
For to such a worthy man as he,
By his way of thinking, it was unseemly
To have any acquaintance with the lowly poor;
It was not respectable and it got him nowhere
To deal with outcasts and the rabble,
Instead of with the rich and sellers of victuals!
And with everyone from whom he could get money
He was as courteous and humble as could be.
There was no other man so virtuous;
He was the best beggar of his house.

Pilgrims set off
on their journey
to Canterbury.

deep and personal experience of religion. Sometimes these people did not find what they were looking for in the established Church. Instead, they turned to religious movements that frequently went against official Christian teachings. The Church called these movements heresies.

The most powerful heresy of the Middle Ages was Catharism, which flourished especially in southern France. Cathars taught that humans were a mixture of spirit and matter; that spirit was created by a good God and that matter and all evils were created by an evil God. It was possible, the Cathars believed, to rise above matter and evil to reach spiritual perfection in this life. Although the Cathars were still Christians, they also taught that Jesus had never really become human. They believed that even in his time on earth he had been completely spiritual. In addition, the Cathars allowed women to play an equal role with men in religion.

Even though most Cathars lived quiet, decent, family-centered lives, the Church found their ideas very dangerous. In the early thirteenth century, the pope sent out many preachers to try to bring the Cathars back to the Church's teachings. When this did not work, the pope allowed the nobles of northern France to mount a crusade against southern France.

This was the first major outbreak of violent intolerance between different groups of European Christians. It was not the last, and it was echoed by new waves of prejudice and violence against Jews, Muslims, and other non-Christians. The Church formed a new office, the Inquisition, dedicated to rooting out heresy and making sure that people followed only accepted teachings.

The rest of the Middle Ages saw many upheavals in the religious life of Europe. Yet through it all, people of faith and good will continued to do what they could to show the love of God in the world. To them, true religion was to connect themselves to the Divine and to the people around them. Perhaps their example can help us today as we continue to learn to understand and accept the beautiful diversity of the human race.

Where there is charity and wisdom
there is neither fear nor ignorance.
—Saint Francis of Assisi

A monk, the cellarer of his monastery, gives in to temptation and helps himself to the wine barrel.

GLOSSARY

abbey   a large monastery headed by an abbot or abbess, the highest rank of monk or nun; an abbey could have a number of other monasteries called priories under its authority

allod   a freeholding, land completely belonging to the family that owns it, with no claims on it by any lord

altarpiece   a painting or carved panel at the back of the altar; it usually showed episodes from the lives of Jesus and the saints

apothecary   a person who made medicines; a pharmacist

apprentice   a student being trained in a craft by a master craftsperson

bailey   a fortified enclosure or castle courtyard

bishop   a high-ranking churchman who oversees religious affairs for a particular region

borough (BUR-oh)   English term for a town to which the king granted the right of self-government, usually in return for an annual tax payment

bourgeois (boorzh-WAH)   French name for a middle-class city dweller

brazier (BRAY-zher)   a portable metal container for a small fire or hot coals

burgesses, burghers   English names for city dwellers, especially those who owned property in a borough, paid part of the borough's annual tax to the king, and enjoyed special privileges and full political rights in the borough

cathedral   a church where a bishop has his headquarters; the word comes from *cathedra*, "throne," because the bishop had his throne, symbolizing his authority, behind the high altar of this church

chapter house   the building where monks or nuns gathered every day to hear the reading of a chapter of their Rule and to conduct monastery business

chivalry   the unwritten code of behavior for the ideal knight, who was expected to be brave, loyal, generous, honest, merciful, polite, respectful to women, faithful to the Church, and strong in the defense of those weaker than he

choleric irritable, easily angered

cleric a man trained as a priest but not necessarily serving in the Church

clerk a priest or, as in *The Canterbury Tales*, a scholar studying for the priesthood

cloister a square or rectangular covered walkway around a garden or open area

commune a group of leading citizens bound together by oath to run their businesses and govern their city without interference from an overlord; in general, a self-governing city

convent common name for a women's monastery

crenellated (KREH-nuh-lay-ted) having battlements with alternating square or rectangular high and low sections

croft the area behind a peasant house and yard, used for vegetable gardening

curtain a thick, high stone wall enclosing a bailey or courtyard

demesne (deh-MAIN) the portion of a manor's farmland that belonged to the lord; the lord received everything that was grown on the demesne

disciple (dih-SY-puhl) a devoted student or follower

donjon (DAHN-juhn; source of our word *dungeon*) or **keep** a stronghold or inner tower; the strongest, inner part of a castle

double monastery a monastery for both men and women, where they lived in separate, neighboring buildings and were ruled by the same superior

dovecote an enclosure for domestic pigeons

dower the part of a man's property—usually one-third to one-half of it—that he pledged to his wife before they married; if the wife outlived her husband, she would have the use of the dower for the rest of her life; when she died, the dower would return to her husband's family

dowry money and other property that a woman brought into marriage

errant (AIR-unt) a knight without land of his own who earned his living by serving a lord for pay; *errant* means "wandering," and errant knights often went from lord to lord and from tournament to tournament, seeking their fortunes

falconry   a form of hunting using trained falcons or hawks to bring down game birds (such as ducks, pheasants, and partridges) and other small animals

fallow   describes land in which no seeds are planted so that it can "rest" and regain its fertility

feudalism (FYOO-duhl-ism)   a military and political arrangement among kings and noblemen, in which a vassal pledged loyalty and military service to an overlord in return for land and protection

fief (FEEF)   the land that a lord granted to his vassal; fiefs could also be other things that brought in income, such as mills, toll bridges, and markets

founder   a craftsperson who makes metal objects by melting the metal and pouring it into molds

friar (from Latin *frater*, "brother")   a monk belonging to the Franciscan or Dominican order

garderobe (GAR-drohb)   an alcove with a kind of toilet seat built over a chute or drainpipe that led to a pit, cellar, ditch, stream, or moat

guild   an organization of people in the same craft or trade; the guild set standards of training and workmanship and looked after its members' interests in various ways

haberdasher   a merchant dealing in small goods

homage (AH-mij)   actions or words that express special honor and respect

Islam   the religion founded by Muhammad in seventh-century Arabia; *Islam* means "submission to God"

keep   *see* donjon

knight   a warrior of the noble class, trained to fight on horseback

lay brother or **lay sister**   a man or woman who took the vows of poverty, chastity, and obedience and lived in a monastery but did the everyday work of the monastery instead of taking part in all the daily religious services

manor   an estate held by a lord, made up of his own land and land held by peasant villagers in exchange for rents and services

manorialism (muh-NOR-ee-uhl-izm)   the arrangement between peasants and their lords, in which peasants held land from the lord and owed him various fees and services in exchange

manuscript   a book produced entirely by hand; manuscripts in the Middle Ages were often illustrated with colorful paintings called illuminations or miniatures

mason   a skilled worker who cut stone into the right shapes for building or constructed the stone walls of a building

Mass   a religious service featuring Holy Communion (the consuming of bread and wine as symbols of the body and blood of Christ)

merchet   the English name for the fee that was paid to the lord when an unfree woman married

mesnie (may-NEE)   the military men of a lord's household

mews   a building that housed falcons and hawks kept for hunting

minstrel   an entertainer who sang and played music, often traveling from place to place

missionary   a person who travels to teach his or her religion to the people of another place

monastery   a community of men or women devoted to prayer, study, and work; also, the buildings housing such a community

motte (MAHT; source of our word *moat*)   an earthen mound, usually surrounded by a ditch, on which a keep was built

Muslim   a follower of the religion of Islam

nave   the main part of a church, where the people gathered to attend religious services

notary   a person who wrote out legal or official documents for individuals; like a modern notary public, a medieval notary could also certify documents to make them official

page   a boy in the first stage of training for knighthood

parchment   sheepskin or goatskin specially prepared for writing on

penance   actions undertaken to show sorrow for and make up for sinful behavior

pilgrimage   a journey to an important religious site, such as a church that houses the remains of a saint

portcullis (port-KUHL-us)   a heavy gate between the gatehouse towers that could be raised and lowered

prowess   skill

refectory   the monastery building where monks and nuns had their meals

rule   a book that gave guidance and rules for monastery life

saint   a person recognized by the Church as being especially holy and able to perform miracles both during life and after death

scutage (SKOO-tij)   money that a vassal paid to a lord instead of performing military service for him

secular (SEH-kyoo-ler)   "in the world," moving among ordinary people and taking part in everyday life

seneschal (SEN-uh-shul)   a high-ranking servant who supervised a lord's household and manors; also called a steward

serf   an unfree peasant, with specific financial and labor obligations to an overlord

sheepfold   a pen for sheep, usually with a shed or barn for the sheep to shelter in

shrine   a place where people pray to one particular saint or other religious figure

squire   a teenage boy who served and learned from a knight for two to four years in preparation for becoming a knight himself

superior   the abbot, abbess, prior, or prioress who was the head of a monastery

tallage   a tax that serfs had to pay to their lord; in some places it was paid every year, and in other places the lord could demand tallage whenever he wished

toft   the yard of an English peasant house

tonsure (TAHN-shur)   a haircut that left the top of the head bald

tournament   a contest or mock battle between groups of knights

trestle table   a table made by laying a large board across two or more supports

trivet   a metal stand used under a hot dish at table

vassal   a noble who held land from a more powerful noble or king in exchange for military service and a pledge of loyalty

villein (vih-LANE)   an unfree peasant; synonymous with *serf*

FOR FURTHER READING

Barter, James. *Life in a Medieval Village*. San Diego: Lucent Books, 2003.

Child, John, et al. *The Crusades*. New York: Peter Bedrick, 1996.

Clare, John D., ed. *Fourteenth-Century Towns*. San Diego: Harcourt Brace, 1993.

Corbishley, Mike. *The Middle Ages*. 3rd ed. New York: Chelsea House, 2007.

Corrain, Lucia. *Giotto and Medieval Art: The Lives and Works of the Medieval Artists*. New York: Peter Bedrick, 1995.

Crossley-Holland, Kevin. *The World of King Arthur and His Court: People, Places, Legend, and Lore*. New York: Dutton, 1999.

Davenport, John. *The Age of Feudalism*. San Diego: Lucent Books, 2007.

Elliott, Lynne. *Medieval Towns, Trade, and Travel*. New York: Crabtree Publishing, 2004.

Findon, Joanne. *Science and Technology in the Middle Ages*. New York: Crabtree Publishing, 2004.

Gravett, Christopher. *The World of the Medieval Knight*. New York: Peter Bedrick, 1996.

Groves, Marsha. *Manners and Customs in the Middle Ages*. New York: Crabtree Publishing, 2006.

Hanawalt, Barbara. *The European World, 400–1400*. New York: Oxford University Press, 2005.

Hinds, Kathryn. *Medieval England*. New York: Benchmark Books, 2002.

———. *Venice and Its Merchant Empire*. New York: Benchmark Books, 2002.

Hunt, Norman Bancroft. *Living in Medieval Europe*. New York: Facts on File, 2008.

Kerr, Daisy. *Medieval Town*. New York: Franklin Watts, 1997.

Langley, Andrew. *Medieval Life*. New York: Knopf, 1996.

Lewis, Naomi, trans. *Proud Knight, Fair Lady: The Twelve Lais of Marie de France*. New York: Viking Kestrel, 1989.

Macauley, David. *Cathedral: The Story of Its Construction*. Boston: Houghton Mifflin, 1973.

————. *Castle*. Boston: Houghton Mifflin, 1977.

Macdonald, Fiona. *A Medieval Cathedral*. New York: Peter Bedrick, 1991.

McAleavy, Tony. *Life in a Medieval Abbey*. New York: Enchanted Lion Books, 2003.

Nardo, Don. *Life on a Medieval Pilgrimage*. San Diego: Lucent Books, 1996.

————. *Lords, Ladies, Peasants, and Knights: Class in the Middle Ages*. San Diego: Lucent Books, 2006.

————. *The Medieval Castle*. San Diego: Lucent Books, 1998.

Osborne, Mary Pope. *Favorite Medieval Tales*. New York: Scholastic Press, 1998.

Peters, Stephanie True. *The Black Death*. New York: Benchmark Books, 2004.

Plain, Nancy. *Eleanor of Aquitaine and the High Middle Ages*. New York: Benchmark Books, 2006.

Steele, Philip. *Castles*. New York: Kingfisher, 1995.

ONLINE INFORMATION

Annenberg Media. *Middle Ages: What Was It Really Like to Live in the Middle Ages?*
http://www.learner.org/interactives/middleages/

BBC. *British History: The Middle Ages.*
http://www.bbc.co.uk/history/british/middle_ages/

Britain Express. *Medieval England.*
http://www.britainexpress.com/History/medieval_britain_index.htm

Camelot International. *Medieval Life.*
http://www.camelotintl.com/village/index.html

Castles on the Web.
http://www.castlesontheweb.com

Gilberts, Rachel. *Medieval Europe.*
http://www.mnsu.edu/emuseum/history/middleages/

McCafferty, James. *Early Music in Schools: Musical Instruments.*
http://www.earlymusic.i12.com/general/music_ix.htm

Metropolitan Museum of Art. *The Timeline of Art History: Medieval Art.*
http://www.metmuseum.org/toah/hi/te_index.asp?i=15

Milot, Marie-Christine. *Paris at the Time of Philippe-Auguste.*
http://www.philippe-auguste.com/uk/

Osborn, Tracey. *The Middle Ages, Chivalry, & Knighthood.*
http://www.teacheroz.com/Middle_Ages.htm

Scheid, Troy, and Laura Toon. *Dominion and Domination of the Gentle Sex: The Lives of Medieval Women.*
http://library.thinkquest.org/12834/

Thomas, Jeffrey L. *Castles of Wales.*
http://www.castlewales.com/home.html

SELECTED BIBLIOGRAPHY

Alsford, Stephen. *Medieval English Towns.* http://www.trytel.com/~tristan/ towns/towns.html

Armstrong, Regis J., and Ignatius C. Brady, trans. *Francis and Clare: The Complete Works.* New York: Paulist Press, 1982.

Atkinson, Clarissa W. *The Oldest Vocation: Christian Motherhood in the Middle Ages.* Ithaca, NY: Cornell University Press, 1991.

Bloch, Marc. *Feudal Society.* Translated by L. A. Manyon. Chicago: University of Chicago Press, 1961.

Brooke, Christopher. *The Monastic World 1000–1300.* New York: Random House, 1974.

Burton, Janet. *Monastic and Religious Orders in Britain 1000–1300.* New York: Cambridge University Press, 1994.

Cantor, Norman F. *The Civilization of the Middle Ages.* New York: Harper Perennial, 1994.

The Catholic Encyclopedia. http://www.newadvent.org/cathen/index.html

Chaucer, Geoffrey. *The Canterbury Tales: A Selection.* Edited by Donald R. Howard. New York: New American Library, 1969.

Cosman, Madeleine Pelner. *Fabulous Feasts: Medieval Cookery and Ceremony.* New York: George Braziller, 1976.

———. *Medieval Holidays and Festivals: A Calendar of Celebrations.* New York: Charles Scribner's Sons, 1981.

Coulton, G. G. *The Medieval Village.* 1925; reprint, New York: Dover, 1989.

DeGregorio, Scott. *Guide to On-line Resources in Medieval Spirituality.* http://www.bede.net/spiritual.html

De Hamel, Christopher. *Medieval Craftsmen: Scribes and Illuminators.* Toronto: University of Toronto Press, 1992.

Duby, Georges. *France in the Middle Ages 987–1460: From Hugh Capet to Joan of Arc.* Translated by Juliet Vale. Cambridge, MA: Basil Blackwell, 1991.

Editors of Time-Life Books. *What Life Was Like in the Age of Chivalry: Medieval Europe AD 800–1500.* Alexandria, VA: Time-Life Books, 1997.

Gies, Frances, and Joseph Gies. *Cathedral, Forge, and Waterwheel: Technology and Invention in the Middle Ages.* New York: HarperCollins, 1994.

———. *Life in a Medieval Castle.* New York: Harper & Row, 1974.

———. *Life in a Medieval City.* New York: Harper Perennial, 1969.

———. *Life in a Medieval Village.* New York: Harper & Row, 1990.

———. *Women in the Middle Ages.* New York: Barnes & Noble, 1978.

Hallam, Elizabeth, ed. *Chronicles of the Crusades: Nine Crusades and Two Hundred Years of Bitter Conflict for the Holy Land Brought to Life through the Words of Those Who Were Actually There.* New York: Weidenfeld and Nicolson, 1989.

Halsall, Paul, ed. *Internet Medieval Sourcebook.* http://www.fordham.edu/halsall/sbook.html

Harbin, Andrea R., ed. *NetSERF: The Internet Connection for Medieval Resources.* http://www.netserf.org

Heer, Friedrich. *The Medieval World: Europe 1100–1350.* Translated by Janet Sondheimer. Cleveland: World Publishing, 1961.

Herlihy, David, ed. *Medieval Culture and Society.* New York: Walker, 1968.

Herlihy, David. *Women, Family, and Society in Medieval Europe: Historical Essays, 1978–1991.* Oxford: Berghahn Books, 1995.

Irvine, Martin, and Deborah Everhart. *The Labyrinth: Resources for Medieval Studies.* http://labyrinth.georgetown.edu

Kelly, Amy. *Eleanor of Aquitaine and the Four Kings.* Cambridge, MA: Harvard University Press, 1950.

Le Roy Ladurie, Emmanuel. *Montaillou: The Promised Land of Error.* Translated by Barbara Bray. New York: George Braziller, 1978.

Loomis, Roger Sherman, and Laura Hibbard Loomis, eds. *Medieval Romances.* New York: Modern Library, 1957.

Luria, Maxwell S., and Richard L. Hoffman, eds. *Middle English Lyrics.* New York and London: W. W. Norton, 1974.

Matterer, James L. *Gode Cookery.* http://www.godecookery.com/godeboke/godeboke.htm

Mertes, Kate. *The English Noble Household 1250–1600: Good Governance and Politic Rule.* New York: Basil Blackwell, 1988.

Metford, J. C. J. *Dictionary of Christian Lore and Legend.* London: Thames and Hudson, 1983.

Milot, Marie-Christine. *Paris sous Philippe-Auguste*. http://www. philippe-auguste.com/

Packard, Sidney R. *12th Century Europe: An Interpretive Essay*. Amherst: University of Massachusetts Press, 1973.

Redon, Odile, Françoise Sabban, and Silvano Serventi. *The Medieval Kitchen: Recipes from France and Italy*. Translated by Edward Schneider. Chicago: University of Chicago Press, 1998.

Riley-Smith, Jonathan, ed. *The Oxford Illustrated History of the Crusades*. New York: Oxford University Press, 1995.

Shahar, Shulamith. *Childhood in the Middle Ages*. Translated by Chaya Galai. New York: Routledge, 1990.

———. *The Fourth Estate: A History of Women in the Middle Ages*. Translated by Chaya Galai. New York: Methuen, 1983.

Talarico, Kathryn, ed. *The ORB: On-line Reference Book for Medieval Studies*. http://www.the-orb.net/index.html

TEAMS Middle English Texts. http://www.lib.rochester.edu/camelot/teams/tmsmenu.htm

Tennant, Roy. *The Online Medieval and Classical Library*. http://omacl.org

Tompkins, Ken. *Wharram Percy, the Lost Medieval Village*. http://loki. stockton.edu/~ken/wharram/wharram.htm

Verheyen, Boniface, OSB, trans. *The Holy Rule of Saint Benedict*. http://www.holyrule.com

INDEX

Page numbers for illustrations are in boldface.

PICTURE CREDITS

Images provided by Rose Corbett Gordon, Art Editor, of Mystic, CT, from the following sources:

Front & back covers: The Pierpont Morgan Library/Art Resource, NY

Page 1: The Art Archive/Victoria and Albert Museum, London/ Graham Brandon; page 5: By permission of the British Library, MS Royal 6.

The Castle Page 6: Private Collection; pages 8, 13, 33, 35: Bibliothèque Nationale, Paris/Bridgeman Art Library; pages 11, 49: Art Resource, NY; pages 15, 41: North Wind Pictures; page16: Lee Snider/The Image Works; page 19: Musée Condé, Chantilly/Index/Bridgeman Art Library; pages 20, 21: Erich Lessing/Art Resource, NY; page 24: The Metropolitan Museum of Art, Gift of John D. Rockefeller Jr., 1937 (37.80.5); pages 28, 52, 68, 70: British Library, London © British Library Board. All Rights Reserved/Bridgeman Art Library; pages 31, 38, 49: Giraudon/Art Resource, NY; pages 36, 37, 56: Private Collection/Bridgeman Art Library; page 45: Mark Antman/The Image Works; page 46: The New York Public Library/Art Resource, NY; page 58: Cliché/Bibliothèque Nationale de France, Paris; page 62: The Pierpont Morgan Library/Art Resource, NY; page 64: Musée des Arts Decoratifs, Paris/Bridgeman Art Library.

The City Page 72: The Bodleian Library, University of Oxford, MS Bodl.264 f.54v; pages 74, 89, 104: Scala/Art Resource, NY; page 79: Galleria dell'Accademia Carrara, Bergamo, Italy/Bridgeman Art Library; pages 81, 95, 100, 120: North Wind Pictures; page 83: Royal

Library of Belgium, Brussels, Chronique de Hainaut, MS 9242 f.274v; pages 86, 88, 110, 117, 118: Cliché/Bibliothèque Nationale de France, Paris; page 91: Musée Condé, Chantilly, France/Roger-Viollet, Paris/Bridgeman Art Library; page 93: Giraudon/Art Resource, NY; pages 97, 130: The Pierpont Morgan Library/Art Resource, NY; page 101: Photothèque des Musées de la Ville de Paris; pages 103, 105: Bibliothèque Nationale, Paris/Bridgeman Art Library; page 109: Biblioteca Estense, Modena, Italy/Bridgeman Art Library; page 113: Archivo Iconographico SA/Corbis; page 116: The Bodleian Library, University of Oxford, MS Laud Misc.751 f.19v; pages 122, 126: British Library, London © British Library Board. All Rights Reserved/Bridgeman Art Library; page 124: Bettmann/Corbis; page 128: Private Collection/Bridgeman Art Library.

The Country Page 134: Corpus Christi College, Oxford/Bridgeman Art Library; pages 136, 161, 184, 196: British Library, London © British Library Board. All Rights Reserved/Bridgeman Art Library; pages 139, 187: Bibliothèque Nationale, Paris/Bridgeman Art Library; pages 141, 170, 193: Giraudon/Art Resource, NY; page 143: Topham/The Image Works; pages 145, 154: North Wind Picture Archives; page 147: The Pierpont Morgan Library/Art Resource, NY; page 149: Photo by John Bethell/Bridgeman Art Library; page 150: Fitzwilliam Museum, University of Cambridge/Bridgeman Art Library International; page 153: The Art Archive/British Library; page 162: British Library/Art Resource, NY; pages 164, 176, 195: Scala/Art Resource, NY; page 167: MS fr.1,t.1,f.22, Bibliothèque Publique Universitaire de Genève/Photo Jean Marc Meylan; page 172: Erich Lessing/Art Resource, NY; page 177: By permission of the British Library; page 179: Christie's Images/Bridgeman Art Library; page 189: Tate Gallery, London/Art Resource, NY; page 191: Private Collection/Bridgeman Art Library.

The Church Pages 198, 263: Topham/The Image Works; page 200: Biblioteca Nazionale, Turin, Italy, Roger-Viollet, Paris/Bridgeman Art Library; page 203: Jewish National & University Library; pages 205, 228: Scala/Art Resource, NY; page 207: Manu Sassoonian/ Art Resource, NY; page 209: David Lees/Corbis; page 212: Erich Lessing/Art Resource, NY; page 214: North Wind Picture Archives; page 217: Peter Willi/Bridgeman Art Library; pages 222, 243, 247, 254: Giraudon/Art Resource, NY; pages 231, 260: British Library, London © British Library Board. All Rights Reserved/Bridgeman Art Library; page 239: Musée de l'assistance publique, Paris; page 240: Smith Art Gallery and Museum, Stirling, Scotland/Bridgeman Art Library; page 249: Pierpont Morgan Library/Art Resource, NY; page 250: Bridgeman Art Library; pages 258, 261: Private Collection/ Bridgeman Art Library; pages 232, 233: Victoria & Albert Museum/Art Resource, NY.

ABOUT THE AUTHOR

Kathryn Hinds grew up near Rochester, NY. She studied music and writing at Barnard College, and did graduate work in comparative literature and medieval studies at the City University of New York. She has written more than thirty books for young people, most recently the four-volume series LIFE IN THE MEDIEVAL MUSLIM WORLD. Kathryn lives in the north Georgia mountains with her husband, their son, and an assortment of cats and dogs. When she is not reading or writing, she enjoys music, dancing, gardening, knitting, and taking walks in the woods. Visit Kathryn online at http://www.kathrynhinds.com.